Imperial Mongolian Cooking
Recipes from
the Kingdoms of Genghis Khan

HIPPOCRENE is NUMBER ONE in International Cookbooks

Africa and Oceania
Best of Regional African Cooking
Egyptian Cooking
Good Food from Australia
Traditional South African Cookery
Taste of Eritrea

Asia and Near East
Afghan Food and Cookery
Best of Goan Cooking
Best of Kashmiri Cooking
Imperial Mongolian Cooking
The Joy of Chinese Cooking
The Art of South Indian Cooking
The Indian Spice Kitchen
The Art of Persian Cooking
The Art of Israeli Cooking
The Art of Turkish Cooking
The Art of Uzbek Cooking

Mediterranean
Best of Greek Cuisine
Taste of Malta
A Spanish Family Cookbook
Tastes of North Africa

Western Europe
Art of Dutch Cooking
Best of Austrian Cuisine
A Belgian Cookbook
Cooking in the French Fashion (bilingual)
Celtic Cookbook
Cuisines of Portuguese Encounters
English Royal Cookbook
The Swiss Cookbook
Traditional Recipes from Old England
The Art of Irish Cooking
Traditional Food from Scotland
Traditional Food from Wales
The Scottish-Irish Pub and Hearth Cookbook
A Treasury of Italian Cuisine (bilingual)

Scandinavia
Best of Scandinavian Cooking
The Best of Finnish Cooking
The Best of Smorgasbord Cooking
Good Food from Sweden

Central Europe
All Along the Rhine
All Along the Danube
Best of Albanian Cooking
Best of Croatian Cooking
Bavarian Cooking
Traditional Bulgarian Cooking
The Best of Czech Cooking
The Best of Slovak Cooking
The Art of Hungarian Cooking
Hungarian Cookbook
Art of Lithuanian Cooking
Polish Heritage Cookery
The Best of Polish Cooking
Old Warsaw Cookbook
Old Polish Traditions
Treasury of Polish Cuisine (bilingual)
Poland's Gourmet Cuisine
Taste of Romania
Taste of Latvia

Eastern Europe
The Cuisine of Armenia
The Best of Russian Cooking
Traditional Russian Cuisine (bilingual)
The Best of Ukrainian Cuisine

Americas
Argentina Cooks
Cooking the Caribbean Way
Mayan Cooking
The Honey Cookbook
The Art of Brazilian Cookery
The Art of South American Cookery
Old Havana Cookbook (bilingual)

Imperial Mongolian Cooking
Recipes from
the Kingdoms of Genghis Khan

by Marc Cramer

HIPPOCRENE BOOKS, INC.
NEW YORK

For information, address:
HIPPOCRENE BOOKS, INC.
171 Madison Avenue
New York, NY 10016

Cataloging-in-Publication Data available from the Library of Congress

Printed in the United States of America.

Acknowledgments

To my family for their unconditional love, faith, and support, and for instilling in me a lingering respect for my heritage, without which this book would not have been possible.

Thanks many times over to my literary agent, Charlotte Gusay, for her enthusiasm and tenacity. I would also like to thank Karen Fraley for her thorough proofreading of the manuscript, and Carol Chitnis, my editor at Hippocrene Books, for championing this book.

Dedication

To His Holiness, the Fourteen Dalai Lama of Tibet-a beacon for humankind in a century of unparalleled violence and darkness.

Photo Credits

Cover photo courtesy of Landsdowne Publishing Pty Ltd, Reg Morrison, photographer. Back jacket art courtesy of the Mongolian State Publishing House, Ulaanbaatar.

Table of Contents

Part 1

INTRODUCTION

In back of the beyond lies a land largely unknown to the West, a place whose very name conjures images of barbarous hordes and bloodthirsty conquests. Surrounded by an aura of fear and fascination, Westerners have written off Mongolia as a brutal and barren land without a culture or cuisine worthy of mention. Yet nothing could be further from the truth.

Imperial Mongolian Cooking: Recipes from the Kingdoms of Genghis Khan is the first ever collection of recipes from a civilization that ruled over some two dozen countries. As such, this book opens a window onto a culture and diverse culinary tradition unknown to the West, offering an original and exciting cooking adventure.

The easy-to-follow recipes that comprise this book are taken from each of the four khanates (or kingdoms) that comprised the greatest empire the world has ever seen, an empire that spanned two continents and lasted nearly four hundred years. The recipes are taken from the various countries that comprised the vast and diverse Mongol Empire: the newly independent and democratized Mongolia, Chinese-controlled Inner Mongolia, China, Tibet (now occupied by the Peoples Republic of China), Azerbaijan, Kyrgyzstan, Tajikistan, Turkmenistan, Uzbekistan, Kazakhstan, Georgia, Armenia, Russia, Poland, The Ukraine, Hungary, Burma, Vietnam, Persia, Iraq, Afghanistan, Syria, and Turkey. Every dish is taken from one of the four khanates that comprised the great Mongol Empire:

* Khanate of the Great Khan—The original empire of Genghis Khan, comprised of Mongolia, Inner Mongolia, Korea, Burma, Vietnam, and northern China.

* Chaghadai Khanate—Named for Genghis Khan's second son, it included Uzbekistan, Tajikistan, Turkmenistan, Kazakhstan, and Kyrgyzstan.

* The Ilkhanate—Originally the domain of Hulegu, grandson of Genghis Khan, the empire incorporated Iraq, Iran, Afghanistan, Turkey, Syria, and Armenia.

* Khanate of the Golden Horde—The last of the four khanates to fall was founded by Batu Khan, Genghis Khan's youngest and

most accomplished son. It lasted into the sixteenth century and included my grandfather's Russia, The Ukraine, Georgia, Poland, and Hungary.

Virtually all the dishes can be made quickly and easily from ingredients available in any supermarket or Asian grocery. A few of the dishes may require some practice and patience, but none are difficult. And virtually all the recipes are surprisingly inexpensive. Mongolian imperial cuisine may be exotic but it is also practical and user-friendly.

The book's origins are a bit more complicated than its culinary offerings. I was born and raised in London as a second generation Briton with roots extending into the soil of East Europe and Central Asia. As war began to foment between Russia and Japan in 1904, my grandfather, a tempestuous Russian of Mongolian ancestry, bored by the restaurant trade and in search of adventure, found himself decked out in the regalia of an officer of the Czar's Imperial Army. Fluent in seven languages, including Mongolian, he was sent to fight against the invading Japanese at Mukden and Liaoyan near the Mongolian-Manchurian border. In charge of training troops stationed in the Russian-dominated Hulan Beir region of Inner Mongolia, he prepared to do battle with the Japanese, the first Asian military force to defeat a European army in over three centuries.

Under my grandfather's command was an audacious Mongol polyglot named Dorje ("Thunderbolt") Gangchen, a former lama and chef in the service of the man who would later become the Bogdo Khan, the last khan of Mongolia. Never one to take his vows of celibacy too seriously, the hapless Dorje made the nearly fatal mistake of a romantic indiscretion with the future khan's wife. Fearing for his life, he fled Mongolia and joined the Russian army, where his culinary skills and capacity to drink any Russian under the table won my grandfather's respect and friendship.

Although hardened to the Russian winters, Grandfather was not prepared for the ferocity of the arctic winds that swept across the Gobi at speeds exceeding 120 m.p.h. He succumbed to typhoid and was sent home to Moscow for medical treatment. Few expected him to survive.

Knowing that on recovery he would be returned to harsh Mongolian climes, Grandfather snuck out of the hospital in the dead of night and bribed a railway worker to sew him into a sack of export grain on a train bound for Poland. The moment the train crossed the Polish border, he cut himself free and made his way to England. There the long arm of the firing squads the Czar reserved for deserters could never reach him.

As Russia fell under communist domination in 1917, my grandfather, now a restaurateur in London, spent his days drinking endless cups of tea from the shiny brass samovar that graced his office. There he delighted in sharing bountiful meals, recipes, and tales of his Mongolia days with his family and circle of fellow expatriates. When I was a child, my grandfather introduced me to the cuisine of the steppes. Many of his recipes were handed down to me. Now it is my turn to share them with you.

Here, then, is the only collection of recipes from the greatest empire the world has even seen. In putting together this collection, I have attempted to open a window to an ancient culture and cuisine unknown to the West.

There is an old saying from my grandfather's country: "Scratch a Russian and you will find a Mongol beneath." Savor its antiquity. Rejoice in its diversity. Celebrate its unique array of tastes and textures.

In a word, enjoy.

Genghis Khan and the Rise and Fall of the Mongol Empire

He was the son of a minor chieftain born in the tempestuous Gobi sometime around 1162. His name was Temujin, "Man of Iron." He would later be known by the title conferred upon him: Genghis Khan.

As a child, Temujin's mother held up a single arrow and snapped it with ease. She then bundled a fistful of arrows and asked the boy to break them, but he could not. A man alone, he learned, could easily be broken. The key to strength was unity. And unity required leadership.

When Temujin's father was murdered by revival tribesmen, the thirteen year old retreated to the forest. Temujin was hunted down and eventually captured. The humiliation of wearing the kang, a heavy wooden yolk that immobilized his hands and arms, only fueled Temujin's determination. Using his native cunning, he soon escaped. Tales of his extraordinary courage quickly spread across the steppes. Soon the fledgling warrior attracted a small but loyal following. As he grew to manhood, so did his influence. He soon set about conquering the various warring tribes and forged them into a nation under one banner, his own.

In 1206 a council of Mongol tribes proclaimed him Genghis Khan, "King of Kings." His armies easily overran the great Moslem Empires and cut into Northern China. By 1222, the Russias fell to the Mongol scimitar. Genghis Khan had crushed every foe that stood in his way.

When he died in 1227, the armies of his sons carried on the Mongol legacy by devastating the finest fighting forces of Christendom, expanding his empire across two continents. It was the largest empire the world would ever see.

As the Mongol Empire grew, it became impossible to govern from one place and was conveniently divided into four khanates, or kingdoms. It is from each of these four khanates that the recipes in this book are drawn.

The most important of the kingdoms was the Khanate of the Great Khan, the nerve center of the Mongol Empire. Its capital was Karakoram in Mongolia, but was later moved to China by Genghis Khan's grandson Khubilai, which earned him the resentment of his subjects, many of whom accused him of betraying his nomadic heritage.

Just as surely as empires rise, so they fall. At first, the Mongols seemed invincible, crushing every foe that stood in their way. Even the army of King Béla IV of Hungary, the finest in Europe, was no match for the Mongols, whom they called "The Devil's Horsemen." Only the death of Ogadei Khan, son and successor of Genghis, forced the Mongols to turn from the gates of Vienna and return to the steppes to elect a new Great Khan.

At first harsh, Mongol rule became increasingly more enlightened. Within a few generations, the great destroyers evolved into great builders and administrators. The capital of the Mongol Empire was called Shang-tu, which the English poet Coleridge translated as Xanadu. This summer capital of Khubilai Khan was a vast administrative and cultural center covering sixteen acres. Its cuisine was not Chinese but distinctly Mongol. While the cookery of Genghis Khan's court was crude, Khubilai Khan dined on delicate crepes filled with finely sliced vegetables smothered in a creamy saffron sauce. Court cookery declined as the fortunes of the Mongol Empire faded after Khubilai's death in 1294. The oldest known Chinese cookbook, the *Yin-shan cheng-yao* ("The Proper Management of Food and Beverages"), was not written until 1503, and then only by order of Oljeitu Khan, a Mongol ruler.

It was not until 1260 under Guyuk Khan, the son of Ogadei's widow, that the Mongols tasted the bitterness of defeat at the hands of Egypt's Mameluke Dynasty. News of their defeat soon spread, forever shattering the myth of Mongol invincibility.

When Khubilai Khan took the throne and moved the empire's capital to China, he sought to do what not even Genghis Khan dared to dream—to create a Mongol navy. Khubilai's attempts to invade Japan ended in a crushing defeat that devastated his armada and his spirit. After his death, the great empire envisioned by Genghis Khan began to crumble.

The last bastion of Mongol power was the Khanate of the Golden Horde, which held Moscow in an iron grip until 1480. And then, like that of any aging warrior, the Mongols' grip rapidly weakened. In 1502, Ivan the Terrible openly defied Mongol authority by refusing to kiss the khan's spurs.

It was the kiss of death for the Mongol Empire.

After the Fall:
Tragedy and Triumph

The only foe to conquer the hordes of Genghis Khan was a former Nepalese prince turned monk—and he did it without raising a sword. His name was Siddartha Guatama, known as the Buddha, the Enlightened One.

The Mongols' first contact with Buddhism came in A.D.1207 when Tibet's rulers avoided invasion by paying tribute to the hordes of the Great Khan. Thirty-two years later, Tibet reneged on its taxes and was invaded by Godan Khan, grandson of Genghis, who eventually sought spiritual instruction from Tibetan lamas and introduced Buddhism to his warriors.

When Khubilai Khan ascended the throne, Mongolia's ties to Buddhism were strengthened through the influence of Chubi, his favorite wife, a Buddhist. Christianity, Islam, Buddhism, and shamanism peacefully coexisted in Mongolia until the sixteenth century when Altan Khan formed an alliance with a monk named Sonam Gyatsho and gave him the title Dalai Lama (Mongolian for "Ocean"). Buddhism was now the national religion. It was to mark the end of the Mongols' warlike ways.

The first Buddhist monastery in Mongolia dates from 1586 and was built from the stones of Karakoram, the former capital of the Mongol Empire. Known as Erdenezuu, it was the heart of Mongolia's spiritual renaissance producing remarkable achievements in philosophy, literature, painting, sculpture, and architecture. Buddhism in Mongolia prospered. At any given time, one-third of the male population could be found in its 750 monasteries. The new lord of Mongolia was the Bogdo Khan ("Holy King"), the Living Buddha who was both head of church and state.

Mongolia's tradition of Living Buddhas began with Zanabazar, a direct descendent of Genghis Khan. Born in 1635, Zanabazar left the steppes at age fourteen to study the Dharma in Lhasa. On his return, Zanabazar invented a new Mongolian script, designed temples, and produced some of the finest religious paintings and sculpture in Asia.

No longer a military power, Mongolia came under Manchu control in the seventeenth century, dividing the country into Outer and Inner Mongolia, the latter incorporated into China. In 1947, the communist Chinese took over Inner Mongolia two years before the rest of China would fall into their hands. Shortly thereafter the Russians stepped in and turned Outer Mongolia into a Soviet puppet. On November 26, 1924, the Mongolian People's Republic was officially declared, making it the first Asian country to fall to communism.

With the unseating of the Bogdo Khan, Mongolia's new khan was a revolution "hero" named Horloyn Choibalsan, who shot or poisoned his political enemies, real and imaginary. Soon the Bogdo Khan met a suspicious end. The Mongolian Buddhist community was now divested of its leadership and reduced to powerlessness, enabling Choibalsan to prevent the search for the Bogdo Khan's reincarnated successor. The stage was now set for one of the most bloodthirsty purges to befall the Buddhist clergy.

By the late 1930s, Choibalsan had 17,000 of Mongolia's clergy declared "enemies of the people" and deported to Siberian labor camps, where they soon perished from starvation. Mongolia's monasteries were systematically looted and razed until only the foundation stones remained to remind Mongolians of a way of life that had stood for centuries.

Russian-trained commissars soon replaced the Dharma with recycled Soviet dogma. Within a few short decades, the communist revolution had all but eradicated the last vestiges of Buddhist tradition, leaving the nation awash in hollow slogans and vodka.

For the next fifty years, Mongolia shared the fate of contemporary Tibet. A handful of elderly former monks kept the religion alive through meetings unknown to even their wives and children. On March 7, 1989, came the turning point when Mikhail Gorbachev announced the departure of the last Soviet troops stationed in the country.

Finally free of Soviet control, a Mongolian movement called il tod ("openness") led to open defiance of the one-party state. By mid-1990, Suhbaatar Square in Ulaanbaatar, the Mongolian capital, filled with angry protesters in the first prodemocracy demonstration in Central Asian history. Shortly thereafter the constitution was revised to grant human rights to all citizens, including freedom of worship. Sixty years after Choibalsan's reign of terror, the first Asian country to embrace communism became the first to discard it.

Lamas now mingle freely with Mongolia's peasants and the fashionably dressed, sophisticated middle class. Even some former Communist Party officials have shaved their heads and entered the newly reconstructed monasteries their predecessors helped destroy.

The transition to democracy has been one of hardship. Now without the support of the East Block, chronic shortages of food, fuel, and raw materials have devastated the economy. With a mere 10,000 tourists trickling into the country annually, Mongolia is hard pressed to find the money it needs to revitalize its culture and restore its monasteries and Buddhist identity.

While some lamaseries are being rebuilt, the majority are struggling to become viable centers of worship and many remain neglected. Without local temples or trained lamas, many rural Mongolians have reestablished Buddhism at a grassroots level by conducting ceremonies in traditional round felt tents known as gers.

Mongolians look back on their years of communism with regret and to Tibet with sadness. The descendents of Genghis Khan have regained their religious freedom, but they are painfully aware of the plight of their Tibetan mentors.

While Mongolian losses under Choibalsan were in the thousands, an estimated million Tibetan have perished under the brutality of the People's Liberation Army. Mongolians may have to endure economic hardships and shortages of basic commodities for years to come, but they do so as a people free to take consolation in the Buddhist faith, a right that has been denied Tibetans since 1959. As one Mongolian academician observed, "On the whole, we are glad we share Tibet's religion, but we are equally glad we no longer share its fate."

Today, Mongolians are sending students to India to study with the Dalai Lama to reintroduce the teachings of the Buddha. Many monasteries are undergoing reconstruction, an expense Mongolia's hard-pressed economy can ill afford. The new Mongolia is determined to reenter the international community as a nation with a strong commitment to human rights. Where monasteries once stood as museums of a forgotten past, the chanting of lamas can once again be heard.

After six decades of Soviet repression, the Mongolian Buddha has been reborn.

SAMPLE MENU I
The Northern Lands

APPETIZER
Momo Shapale with Sipen Mardur Sauce
Delicate steamed Tibetan mushroom ravioli smothered in a creamy, spicy yogurt sauce

Sample
Menus

SALAD
Eze
Bhutanese chili and cheese salad

ENTREE
Shabril with Dresil
Tibetan meatball curry with nutted saffron rice, honey, and currants

BREAD
Trimomo
Himalayan steamed bread with turmeric

BEVERAGE
Chang
Tibetan barley beer with honey

DESSERT
Peking Dust
Chinese chestnut mound with cream and glazed fruits

SAMPLE MENU II
The Southern Lands

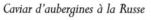

APPETIZER

Caviar d'aubergines à la Russe
Russian eggplant caviar with green and red peppers

SOUP

Borshch Unkrainsky
Ukrainian beet and vegetable soup served with sour cream

ENTREE

Shashlyk with Tkemeli Sauce and Turkman Plov
Marinated Georgian lamb kabobs smothered in a tangy plum sauce
and served over a bed of Turkmenistan-style rice

BREAD

Non
Savory Uzbek flat onion bread

BEVERAGE

Kvass
Russian black bread beer with sultanas

DESSERT

Samsa
Delicate fried walnut fritters from legendary Samarkand

Part II

Appetizers

Russian Eggplant Caviar
Caviar d'aubergines à la Russe
(KHANATE OF THE GOLDEN HORDE)

Perhaps the most famous Russian *zakuski* (hors d'oeuvre) is chilled caviar garnished with lemon and served on small squares of black bread. Equally tempting and far more economical is *caviar d'aubergines*, a traditional Russian spread made from roasted eggplants and bell peppers. It is best served chilled on small squares of black bread.

Appetizers

> *2 to 3 medium eggplants*
> *8 tablespoons olive oil*
> *1 white onion, finely chopped*
> *1 green bell pepper, seeded and finely chopped*
> *1 clove garlic, finely chopped*
> *3 medium tomatoes, peeled, seeded, and finely chopped*
> *salt and ground white pepper, to taste*
> *1 teaspoon paprika*
> *2 tablespoons lemon juice, freshly squeezed and strained*

SERVES 10 TO 12.

Preheat the oven to 400 degrees F for 10 minutes.

Remove the stems and hulls from the eggplant. Brush lightly with a teaspoon of olive oil and bake for an hour, turning at regular intervals. When it is cool, remove the pulp and discard the seeds. Chop finely and set aside.

Heat 4 tablespoons of olive oil in a heavy saucepan. Stir in the onion and cook until transparent. Add the green bell pepper and garlic, cooking over low heat and stirring gently for 5 minutes.

In a large mixing bowl, pound the eggplant pulp and stir in the green pepper mixture. Add the tomatoes, salt, pepper, and paprika.

Add the remaining 4 tablespoons of olive oil to the saucepan over moderate heat. Spoon the eggplant mixture into the oil and raise the heat to a gentle boil, stirring constantly. Cook uncovered for an hour or until all the liquid has evaporated.

Stir in the lemon juice, allow to cool, and chill. Serve over squares of black rye bread.

Steamed Mushroom Dumplings

Momo Shapale

(KHANATE OF THE GREAT KHAN)

Appetizers

If any one meal could be called the national dish of Tibet, it would be *momo*. Whenever there is a feast or celebration in Lhasa, *momo* is served. The most common filling is yak, a meat similar to lean beef. My grandfather found that mushrooms blend beautifully with the combination of vegetables and spices that make up the filling.

Momo can be cooked in any flat steamer, or can be baked or fried. It is equally good as a main meal or as an appetizer.

FILLING:

> 1/3 cup hot water
> 1 cup finely chopped celery
> 1/2 cup chopped green onions
> salt and black pepper, to taste
> 1/2 teaspoon ground cumin
> 1/2 teaspoon ground nutmeg
> 1 teaspoon grated ginger
> 1 1/2 pounds fresh mushrooms, coarsely chopped

DOUGH:

> 3 cups all-purpose flour
> 3 cups whole-wheat flour
> 1 teaspoon baking soda

SERVES 10 TO 12.

In a large mixing bowl, blend the hot water with the celery, green onions, salt, pepper, and the spices. Add the chopped mushrooms. Mix thoroughly.

Using a separate mixing bowl, combine the flours and baking soda. Add enough water to make the dough stiff. Break off a small chunk of dough and roll into a ball about 3/4 inch. Flatten it slightly and dust with flour. Push a rolling pin across the dough, then push the dough from the edge to the middle. Do the same from the opposite side until the dough becomes a 4-inch circle that is slightly thicker in the middle.

Put a teaspoon of filling in the center of the dough. Fold into a half-moon shape. Firmly pinch the edges together. Bend the *momo* holding your thumb in the middle and pinch the edge to reseal.

Brush the bottom and sides of a steamer with vegetable oil. Place all the *momo* in the steamer so that they neither touch each other nor the sides of the steamer. This will prevent them from sticking. In the steamer, bring the water (6 to 9 cups, depending on the size) to a boil, cover tightly, and allow the *momo* to cook for 10 to 15 minutes.

Momo is best served with the spicy Tibetan sauce of your choice.

Variation:
Instead of mushrooms, fill the *momo* with 1 1/2 pounds of ground chicken.

Chickpea Dip With Pureed Sesame Seeds

Hummus

(The Ilkhanate)

A favorite throughout the Islamic world, this version comes from Syria, where the best hummus and Arab pastries originate. While plying his trader of Asian carpets, my Great Uncle Ilya returned from his journeys with as many recipes as rugs, proudly proclaiming his discovery the best version ever. One taste of traditional Syrian hummus, made according to this thirteenth-century recipe, may prove him right.

> *1 cup dried chickpeas*
> *1 teaspoon salt*
> *1/2 cup freshly squeezed lemon juice (about 3 lemons)*
> *1/3 cup tahini (sesame seed sauce)*
> *2 to 3 cloves garlic, crushed*
> *1 tablespoon olive oil*
> *1 teaspoon paprika*

Serves 10 to 12.

Soak the chickpeas overnight in a plastic or ceramic bowl with 3 cups of water. The next day, boil gently for 3 hours, adding the salt during the last hour. Remove from the heat, drain, and allow to cool. Press the chickpeas through a sieve with a little cold water to remove the skins. Place in a non-metal bowl and add the lemon juice and tahini, stirring to blend well.

Stir in the garlic until the mixture is smooth and creamy. Chill and transfer to a ceramic serving dish. Smooth the surface and drizzle with the oil. Dust with paprika and serve with any Middle Eastern bread, such as pita.

Feta Cheese Blended With Spices and Paprika

Korozott Juhturobol

(KHANATE OF THE GOLDEN HORDE)

Appetizers

Though never officially a part of the Mongol Empire, Hungary's history is interwoven with the Mongols. When the forces of Genghis Khan's successors invaded Europe, the army of King Béla IV was consider the finest in Europe and Christendom's last hope against the storm from the East. Although the Hungarians fought bravely, they were no match for the Mongols, now a stone's throw from the gates of Vienna. Leaving the Hungarian plains littered with the fallen Christian knights, word reached the Mongol commanders that Ogadei, Genghis Khan's son and heir to the throne, just died. The Mongols retreated to Karakoram to elect a new Great Khan. Europe was saved.

1 1/4 pounds feta cheese
1/2 pound butter
1/2 pound ricotta
1 teaspoon ground caraway seeds
1 teaspoon dry mustard
1 tablespoon paprika
1/4 teaspoon salt
1/2 teaspoon finely ground black pepper
1/2 cup palenkas (Hungarian apricot brandy) or plain brandy
1/4 cup dark beer
2 spring onions, green part only, chopped
1 red pepper, cut into thin strips

SERVES 10 TO 12.

In a plastic mixing bowl, blend the feta, butter, and ricotta into a smooth paste. When the mixture is creamy, add the caraway seeds, mustard, paprika, salt, and pepper and blend thoroughly. Drizzle in the brandy followed by the beer, stir until the mixture is blended nicely.

-CONTINUED-

Transfer to a glass or ceramic bowl and chill for 2 hours, enabling the beer to lightly ferment the mixture and the texture to become firmer.

Serve sprinkled with the green onions and red pepper.

Spread on cubes of toast or mini-rounds of French bread and serve.

Vietnamese Fried Crab

Cua Rang Muoi

(KHANATE OF THE GREAT KHAN)

Even parts of Vietnam fell to the mighty Mongol armies. Today, Mongols, now Tantric Buddhists, consider fish (or shellfish) a lowly form of life to be shunned. While the Mongols of Genghis Khan's day seldom ate fish, the young Temujin evaded his captors by surviving in the wilderness and eating whatever he could, including fish and crustacean alike.

Appetizers

> *2 pounds fresh crab claws*
> *4 tablespoons oil*
> *4 cloves garlic, finely chopped*
> *4 teaspoons tomato paste*
> *soy sauce to taste*
> *2 green onions, coarsely chopped*

SERVES 4 TO 6.

Using a wooden mallet, crack open the crab claws or pry them open with a sturdy knife. Chop the crabmeat. Meanwhile, heat the oil until hot but not smoking. Stir in the garlic and cook for 1 minute, then add the tomato paste, reducing the heat and stirring for an additional minute.

To this aromatic base add the crabmeat and the soy sauce. Cover tightly, reduce to a simmer, and let the mixture cook for around 5 minutes, stirring every minute to make sure the crab claw cooks evenly.

Transfer to a warm serving dish and sprinkle with green onions.

Spiced Korean Grilled Beef

Bulgogi

(KHANATE OF THE GREAT KHAN)

Appetizers

Genghis Khan's greatest general was Subudei, an intense man and brilliant tactician who forced Korea into submission in 1218. Knowing their army was no match for Subudei's warriors, the Koreans readily recognized Genghis Khan as their overlord and bought off the Mongols with lavish gifts and tribute. The fiercely independent Koreans soon rose up against the Mongols. In 1231, four years after the death of Genghis Khan, Ogadei's forces quashed the Korean's rebellion, leaving behind seventy officials who soon came to savor the delights of *bulgogi* (or "fire meat"). This version was my grandfather's favorite appetizer, one he reserved for parties for his inner circle of Russian expatriates. The heat of the small, fiery beef cubes was extinguished with dousings of chilled vodka.

> *1 pound lean steak*
> *1 tablespoon black sesame seeds*
> *2 cloves garlic, finely chopped*
> *1/4 cup mushroom soy sauce*
> *3/4 teaspoon sugar*
> *2 teaspoons black sesame oil*
> *1 teaspoon red chili oil*
> *1 teaspoon grated ginger*
> *1 teaspoon paprika*
> *1 to 2 teaspoons sherry*
> *1/2 cup chopped green onions*
> *1/2 cup finely sliced radishes*

SERVES 10 TO 12.

Cut the steak across the grain into 1/4-inch slices, then chop into 1 1/2-inch cubes. Set aside. In an unoiled heavy pan, gently toast the sesame seeds to bring out their full, rich flavor. Set aside to cool, then crush. In a plastic, glass, or ceramic bowl, mix the seeds with the garlic, soy, sugar, oils, and the other spices, using the sherry to bind the ingredients.

Stir the beef into the spicy paste, cover, refrigerate and marinate for 4 to 6 hours, turning occasionally. When marinated, place the beef cubes on skewers and cook over a barbecue, hibachi, or an indoor grill for 4 minutes, turning every minute to ensure that the meat cooks evenly and is not overdone.

Place on a warm serving dish and garnish with the chopped green onions and radishes.

Stuffed Grape Leaves
Dolma
(THE ILKHANATE)

Armenian cookery represents the cross-pollination of Christian and Islamic traditions, although it generally leans more toward the Middle Eastern culinary heritage than to western Europe. By the middle of the thirteenth century, Armenia had forged military and political links with the Great Khan, now the bibulous Guyuk Khan, who reigned for two years before dying in 1248. Although the Mongols never adopted the eating of *dolma*, which are popular throughout the Near East, many Russians did, including my family. They adapted the original recipe with characteristic flair—and a few Ukrainian touches.

> *2 cups finely chopped red onions*
> *1/2 cup uncooked long-grain white rice*
> *2 tablespoons unsalted shelled pistachios*
> *2 tablespoons finely chopped dried apricots*
> *1 tablespoon finely chopped fresh parsley*
> *1 tablespoon crushed dried dill*
> *5 tablespoons olive oil*
> *2 tablespoons butter, melted*
> *3 tablespoons lemon juice, freshly squeezed and strained*
> *1 1/2 tablespoons honey*
> *salt and white pepper, to taste*
> *2 tablespoons paprika*
> *1 pound jar grapevine leaves*
> *1 1/4 cups white wine or Crimean champagne*

SERVES 10 TO 12.

In a large plastic or ceramic mixing bowl, blend the onions with the rice, pistachios, apricots, parsley, and dill. Drizzle in the olive oil, butter, lemon juice, and honey. Stir with a wooden spatula and season with salt and pepper. Add the paprika and stir until blended.

Rinse the grapevine leaves in warm water to remove the brine, then set aside to drain on paper towels. Line the bottom of a large casserole dish with ten of the leaves, then use the remaining leaves to hold the stuffing.

Take a teaspoon of the mixture and place it in a leaf a little toward the stem. Then fold the stem over the stuffing. Fold the sides to keep the stuffing in, then roll the leaf forward to form a cigar-shaped cylinder. Place the leaves, seam side down, in the casserole dish and add the white wine.

Cover and slowly bring to a boil, then reduce the heat to low and allow the *dolma* to gently simmer for an hour. Add a little more wine, if necessary.

Remove from the heat onto a wooden board and allow to cool. Refrigerate overnight and serve with thin slices of lemon and a sprinkling of paprika.

Lamb Filled Pancakes

Hushuur à la Tsendjav

(KHANATE OF THE GREAT KHAN)

This recipe is usually served as a main dish in Mongolian restaurants in Ulaanbaatar, but this version hails from Chinese-controlled Inner Mongolia, where it can be served as a delicious appetizer. While the Chinese shy away from lamb preparations, Mongolians and Central Asians use the meat as the staple of their diet.

This easy to make but somewhat exotic version was said to have been a favorite of Tsendjav, the mother of the last khan, who insisted Dorje prepare this rare version of *hushuur*. Those who don't care for lamb may substitute lean beef or even venison.

> 3 tablespoons soy or mushroom soy sauce
> 2 teaspoons sugar
> 1 tablespoon sherry
> 2 teaspoons finely ground white pepper
> 1 tablespoon finely chopped garlic
> 2 1/2 tablespoons cornstarch
> 1 pound ground lamb
> 3 tablespoons finely chopped green onion
> 6 tablespoons oil
> 2 to 3 tablespoons vegetable broth
> 1 tablespoon paprika

SERVES 10 TO 12.

Using a nonmetal mixing bowl, blend the soy, sugar, sherry, pepper, garlic, 1 1/2 tablespoons of the cornstarch, the lamb, and green onion. Mix well and allow to stand an hour for the flavors to blend.

Take the meat and roll it into 12 ping-pong size balls. Flatten with a wooden pastry roller lightly brushed with oil to prevent sticking. Roll into small, flat circles.

In a large skillet or wok, heat the oil over moderate heat. Do not allow the oil to smoke as this will make the mixture cook too quickly and destroy the taste and texture of the dish. Cook the meat patties on both sides until brown. Turn up the heat, add the vegetable broth mixed with the remaining 1 tablespoon of cornstarch to thicken. Reduce the heat to a simmer until done.

Dust with paprika and serve piping hot.

Russian Meatballs
Katuski
(KHANATE OF THE GOLDEN HORDE)

Appetizers

Often prepared for snacks, *katuski* can be served hot or cold. My preference is for piping hot *katuski* on cocktail skewers served with thin slices of black rye bread. Traditionally, *katuski* are made from a mixture of meats including beef, veal, and pork. The following recipe uses ground chicken, although veal can be substituted. My grandfather developed this simple but tasty recipe during World War II when veal was scarce.

> *1/2 cup lemon juice, freshly squeezed and strained*
> *2 pounds ground chicken, preferably breast meat*
> *2 medium onions, finely chopped*
> *1/2 cup butter*
> *4 slices stale French bread*
> *salt and black pepper, to taste*
> *paprika*

SERVES 10 TO 12.

In a large nonmetal mixing bowl add the lemon juice to the chicken and mix thoroughly. Set aside. Fry the onions in the butter until transparent. Soak the bread in water while the onions are cooking. After 5 minutes squeeze the water from the slices and stir them into the chicken along with salt and pepper and onions. Form the chicken mixture into meatballs about the size of golf balls.

Add a little more butter to the pan. Gently fry the meatballs for 25 minutes, stirring frequently to prevent sticking and to ensure that the *katuski* cook evenly.

Dust with paprika and serve.

Soups

Beet And Vegetable Soup

Borshch Unkrainsky

(Khanate of the Golden Horde)

The rich, fertile soil of the Ukraine is known as *chornozem*, or "black earth." Once called the "Breadbasket of the Russias," the Ukraine was conquered by Mongols in the thirteenth century. With the death of Berdebek Khan in 1359, the power of the Golden Horde slipped into gradual decline until the last vestiges of Mongol rule were erased by Ivan the Terrible in 1502.

Soups

4 medium tomatoes
4 tablespoons vegetable oil
1 cup finely chopped onions
2 cloves garlic, finely chopped
2 cups coarsely grated beets
1 cup peeled and coarsely grated celery root
1 cup peeled and coarsely grated parsnips
1 leek, cut into 1/4-inch sections
1 pound potatoes, peeled and cut into 1 1/2-inch cubes
1/2 teaspoon sugar
juice of 1/2 lemon, strained
6 peppercorns
1 bay leaf
1 tablespoon salt
6 to 8 cups beef stock
1 pound cabbage, cored and coarsely shredded
1/2 cup red wine
2 tablespoons tomato puree
3 tablespoons finely chopped parsley
1cup sour cream

SERVES 10 TO 12.

Drop the tomatoes in boiling water for 12 seconds. Then run them under cold water and peel. Remove the stems and cut the tomatoes in half. Squeeze gently to draw out the juices. Discard the seeds and chop coarsely.

Heat the oil and add the onions and garlic, stirring constantly for 5 to 7 minutes. Stir in the beets, celery root, parsnip, half the tomatoes, leek, potatoes, sugar, lemon juice, peppercorns, bay leaf, salt, and the stock. Bring to a boil. Reduce the heat, cover, and simmer for 30 minutes.

Add the cabbage, wine, and tomato puree and cook for 10 minutes. Then stir in the remaining tomatoes, simmering for 10 minutes.

Remove from the heat, pour into bowls and sprinkle with parsley. Add a dollop of sour cream to each diner's bowl and serve.

Mongolian Noodle Soup
Gyatuk
(Khanate of the Great Khan)

A hardy, sustaining combination of noodles and broth, Mongolians often eat their own version of this recipe (known locally as *guriltai shol*) for breakfast. The dish, which is always made with lamb in Mongolia, is known to Tibetans as *gyatuk*, and is prepared with yak meat. Westerners can substitute lean beef or buffalo.

2 tablespoons vegetable oil
1/2 teaspoon fenugreek seeds
3 cloves garlic, finely minced
1 teaspoon powdered ginger
1 pound lean cubed beef
1/2 teaspoon cumin
1/2 teaspoon turmeric
salt to taste
1 pound flat egg noodles
1 cup green onions chopped
1/2 cup thinly sliced onions
1/2 cup thinly sliced tomatoes

SERVES 10 TO 12.

Heat the oil in a heavy pan and stir in the fenugreek seeds until they turn dark brown. Stir in the garlic and ginger. Add the meat, cumin, and turmeric, stirring until the meat is browned. Reduce the heat, add the salt, cover and simmer for 5 minutes. Add 7 cups of water, cover, and cook for 10 minutes.

In a large pot, boil water and add the noodles, cooking until they are tender. Drain off the water and moisten the noodles with a little butter or oil. Place enough noodles in each diner's bowl to fill halfway. Ladle the broth over the noodles and add the green onion, onion slices, and tomatoes.

Imperial Mongolian Cooking

Marrow Bone Soup With Egg

Ruetang

(Khanate of the Great Khan)

The harshness of Tibetan winters is dwarfed by Mongolia's bone-chilling cold season. When the Thirteenth Dalai Lama took political asylum in Mongolia in 1904, even he found the winters unbearably cold. A hearty bowl of *ruetang* makes a nourishing meal that will take the chill out of any winter's day.

Soups

3 pounds marrow bones, chopped into small pieces
4 eggs, beaten
2 teaspoons salt
1 tablespoon soy sauce
1/2 cup finely chopped cilantro

Serves 10 to 12.

Place the bones in 15 cups of water and bring to a boil. Reduce the heat and simmer uncovered for 45 minutes. Remove the bones from the pot. Add the beaten eggs, salt, and soy sauce. Stir well, then add the cilantro. Stir again and serve.

Himalayan Nettle Soup
Satuk
(Khanate of the Great Khan)

For many years the Tibetan poet and spiritual leader Milaraspa lived in a cave above the Kyirong Valley, sustaining himself solely on soup made from local nettles. Tibetans say this is why he is always depicted in religious paintings with green skin. If nettles (sometimes available in dried form) are not available, try substituting chopped spinach. The results are very good, if less exotic.

2 pounds nettles or spinach leaves, chopped
10 cups lamb or beef broth
1 teaspoon crushed ginger
salt to taste
1 teaspoon dried red chili pepper
1 tablespoon all-purpose flour
1 cup milk

Serves 10 to 12.

Use only the tops of young nettle plants. Wash the nettles well using gloves as the plants are notoriously prickly. Cut off and discard the stems. Bring the meat broth to a boil and add the nettles. Add the ginger, salt, and red chili pepper. Reduce the heat and simmer for 30 minutes. Puree the mixture in a blender and return to the cooking pot.

Dissolve the flour in the milk and stir into the soup. Heat until the soup becomes thick and creamy.

Serve piping hot.

Dumpling Soup

Boetuk

(Khanate of the Great Khan)

Here's another sustaining dish from Tibet, the highest country in the world. Traditionally made from yak meat, beef is an excellent substitute. *Boetuk* is often the specialty of cooks called *gyal se machem*, or master chefs. Tibetan chefs must work for years as an apprentice before reaching the status of master chef. *Boetuk* uses a number of ingredients and it requires a touch of patience to make. The results are well worth the extra effort.

Soups

8 cups water or vegetable broth
3 pounds soup bones
2 tablespoons vegetable oil
1/2 teaspoon fenugreek seeds
1 tablespoon finely chopped garlic
1/2 cup sliced onions
1 cup diced tomatoes
1 tablespoon finely chopped ginger
1/2 teaspoon ground nutmeg
1/2 teaspoon ground turmeric
1 pound lean beef, cut into 1-inch cubes
3 teaspoons soy sauce
salt to taste
2 cups finely sliced radishes
1 cup green peas
3 cups whole-wheat flour
3 cups all-purpose flour
1/2 cup finely chopped green onions

SERVES 10 TO 12.

Bring 15 cups of water to a boil, add the bones and simmer for 30 minutes. In a separate pan, heat the oil and add the fenugreek seeds, stirring until they turn dark brown. Then add the garlic and sliced onion, stirring until lightly browned.

-CONTINUED-

Imperial Mongolian Cooking

Add the tomatoes, ginger, nutmeg, and turmeric. Stir gently. Cover and cook over medium heat for 1 minute. Add the meat, soy sauce, and salt, stirring gently to blend. Cover and cook for 20 minutes, adding a little water if the mixture becomes too thick. Stir in the radishes and peas. Cook for 2 minutes.

While the soup is cooking, make the dumplings. Blend the flours and water to make a stiff dough. Roll into a cigar-shaped piece the width of your index finger. Cut into 1/2-inch pieces and sprinkle lightly with flour.

Remove the bones and strain. Add the strained broth to the meat mixture. Bring to a boil and add the dumplings, cooking for 7 to 8 minutes.

Add the green onions and serve right away.

Chicken and Vegetable Soup

Tukpa

(KHANATE OF THE GREAT KHAN)

In Tibet there are dozens of variations of *tukpa*. The version included here makes use of chicken instead of beef or lamb. In the provinces, wide and rather chewy noodles are used. This version adopts the Lhasa style using fine noodles to lend a more delicate texture to this traditional Tibetan dish.

Soups

1 chicken, chopped into pieces and boned
3 bay leaves, whole
1 onion, finely chopped
salt to taste
2 teaspoons minced ginger
4 tablespoons cornstarch
5 cloves garlic, finely minced
1 teaspoon turmeric
4 tablespoons finely chopped cilantro
1 tablespoon sesame oil
12 ounces narrow egg noodles
3 cups chopped bok choy
1 cup sliced celery
2 1/2 cups chopped spinach
1 tablespoon crushed red chili pepper, or to taste

SERVES 12 TO 15.

Bring 12 cups water to a boil and add the meat, bay leaves, onion, salt, and ginger. Cover and simmer for 90 minutes. Mix the cornstarch into 1/2 cup of water. Then mix the garlic, turmeric, and cilantro with the sesame oil in a separate pan. Remove the bay leaves from the cooking pot.

Stir in the noodles and cook for a few minutes. Add the bok choy and celery and cook for 5 minutes until the noodles are almost tender but not quite done. Stir in the cornstarch mixture. Add the spinach when the soup begins to thicken.

Heat the chili in the sesame oil mixture for 1 minute, stir into the soup and serve steaming hot.

Lamb and Tofu Soup

Honiny Mah Shol

(KHANATE OF THE GREAT KHAN)

With the gradual weakening of the Mongol Empire, the Russians and Chinese began to vie for power over the land of their former conquerors. One half of Mongolia fell under Soviet control in 1921, while the southernmost region, known as Inner Mongolia, came under Manchu control after the Chinese defeated Mongol's forces in 1732. Inner Mongolia was absorbed into China, while the Manchus were content to leave Outer Mongolia to its own devices, paving the way for full-blown Russian incursion.

As a rule, the Chinese disdain lamb and believe its fragrance permeates everything cooked in their woks. When one finds lamb on the menu of a Chinese restaurant, the dish most likely originates from Inner Mongolia.

STOCK:

> *1 pound lean lamb*
> *1 leek, whole*
> *1/4 cup dried mushrooms, presoaked for 20 minutes*
> *1/2 teaspoon salt*
> *1 teaspoon soy sauce*

SOUP:

> *1/2 teaspoon cornstarch*
> *2 tablespoons soy sauce*
> *1 cup sliced mushrooms*
> *1 pint firm tofu, diced*
> *1/2 teaspoon salt, or to taste*
> *1/2 to 1 teaspoon crushed red chili pepper, or to taste*
> *1/2 pound cooked lamb, thinly sliced*

SERVES 10 TO 12.

Trim the fat from 1 pound of lamb. Place in a saucepan with 8 cups of cold water and bring to a boil. Add the leek and the mushrooms along with the strained soaking liquid. Reduce the heat and skim the surface. Then cover and let the stock simmer for 30 minutes. Add the salt and soy sauce and cook for another 5 minutes. Remove the meat and the vegetables, strain the stock, and skim off the fat.

For the soup, heat the stock. Just before it boils, add all the mushrooms and stir. Boil for 2 minutes and add the tofu. Boil for another minute and add the salt, red chili pepper, and 1 tablespoon soy sauce. Add the sliced lamb and boil for 5 minutes. Mix 1/2 teaspoon of cornstarch and the remaining 1 tablespoon soy sauce. Add to the broth, stir, and cook for 3 minutes or until the soup thickens.

Stir and serve as a first course.

Yogurt Soup with Barley
Tanabaour
(THE ILKHANATE)

Variations of this recipe can be found throughout the former Mongol Empire, including the Russias where it is usually served in summer. Sustaining and nutritious, it was often prepared with rice when someone in my family was ailing—just the thing for winter colds.

1 cup pearl barely
8 cups beef broth
salt to taste
3 tablespoons vegetable oil
1 large onion, finely chopped
4 tablespoons finely chopped fresh mint
4 tablespoons finely chopped parsley
2 to 3 cups plain yogurt
2 eggs, beaten

SERVES 8.

Wash the barley then soak it in water overnight. Drain. Bring the beef broth to a boil in a heavy cooking pot. Stir in the barley and salt. Reduce the heat and let it simmer uncovered for 45 minutes.

While the barley is cooking, heat the oil and sauté the onion until golden brown. Remove from the heat and stir in the mint and parsley. Add the mixture to the soup.

Place the yogurt in a bowl and stir. Beat in the eggs. Add a few tablespoons of broth, stirring constantly. Make sure the heat is low and stir the yogurt mixture into the soup. Stir constantly until the yogurt is blended in. Do not allow to boil.

Serve with warm bread.

Lentil Soup
Vosbabour
(The Ilkhanate)

Lentil soup is enjoyed throughout Armenia and the Caucasus. It is sometimes made with equal portions of lentils and bulghur wheat. Chicken broth is often substituted for beef, or it can be made with vegetable stock or water. Either way, the soup will be delicate and subtle.

Soups

> *2 cups dried lentils*
> *2 to 3 tablespoons vegetable oil*
> *2 large onions, thinly sliced*
> *9 cups beef broth*
> *2 bay leaves, whole*
> *1 tablespoon paprika*
> *salt to taste*
> *1 teaspoon red chili pepper, or to taste*
> *4 tablespoons finely chopped fresh tarragon*

SERVES 10 TO 12.

Wash the lentils in cold water. In a heavy pot, heat the oil and sauté the onions until transparent, but not brown. Stir in the lentils and cook for an additional 3 minutes. Add the broth, bay leaves, paprika, salt, and red chili pepper. Reduce the heat and cover. Simmer for 20 to 40 minutes, or until the lentils are soft. Remove the bay leaves and puree the soup in a blender until thick and creamy.

Return to the heat and cook on low temperature for 4 or 5 minutes, stirring constantly. Sprinkle with tarragon and serve with warm bread.

Bean and Meatball Soup

Maushawa

(The Ilkhanate)

Dating back to the invasion of Genghis Khan, this dish is often served before the main course in Afghanistan. In this Moslem country, hospitality is a way of life, not merely good manners. Food, which is based around lamb from Asassi fat-tailed sheep, is always eaten with the right hand. Yellow split peas are added to Afghan soups to thicken them, while chili and other spices are used liberally to add zest and vitality.

> *1/2 cup dried red beans*
> *1/2 cup yellow split peas*
> *1/2 cup mung beans*
> *1/2 cup long-grain rice*
> *2 teaspoons salt*

> *Meatballs:*
> *8 ounces finely ground beef or lamb*
> *1/2 teaspoon salt*
> *1/2 teaspoon finely ground black pepper*
> *1/4 teaspoon red chili pepper, or to taste*
> *1/2 teaspoon ground cinnamon*
> *1/2 cup vegetable oil*
> *1 large onion, finely chopped*
> *1/2 cup chopped tomatoes*
> *1 tablespoon finely chopped fresh dill*
> *1 cup plain yogurt*

> *Serves 8 to 10.*

Soak the beans overnight in a nonmetal container. In a large cooking pot, place the red beans and the soaking water. Boil, then reduce the heat and simmer, covered, for 1 hour. Meanwhile, wash the yellow spit peas and the mung beans in cold water. Add to the pot with 2 cups of water and simmer for 30 minutes. Wash the rice until the runoff water is clear and add to the pot with 2 teaspoons of salt, simmering for an additional 30 minutes.

In the mixing bowl, combine the meat with the salt and spices. Shape into 1/2-inch balls. Heat the oil in a separate pan and fry the onion until lightly browned. Add the meatballs and stir gently until browned. Stir in 1/2 cup of water and the tomatoes. Cover and simmer for 30 minutes.

Stir the meat mixture into the bean mixture with 2 additional cups of water and the dill. Bring to a boil. Reduce the heat and stir in the yogurt, making sure it does not boil. If the soup becomes too thick, add water to dilute.

Serve piping hot with warm bread.

Salads

Armenian Salad

Hazar Aghtsan
(THE ILKHANATE)

Mongolia is a vast arid land. Vegetables are now grown in hothouses, but salads have never been a significant part of Mongol diet. Although young Genghis Khan survived in the wilderness living on berries, wild onions, and garlic, nomadic Mongols generally scorn the use of vegetables. An old saying proclaims, "Grass (vegetables) is for animals and meat is for men." Today's Mongolian youth are eating more vegetables than their parents, to whom salads are virtually unknown.

On the other hand, the Mongol's old vassals, the Armenians, love salads. Here is a traditional Armenian salad that that was a favorite in our original Moscow restaurant.

8 cups torn lettuce leaves
1/2 cup peeled, thinly sliced cucumber
1/4 cup sliced green onions, white and green parts
1/4 cup finely chopped mint leaves
1/4 cup finely chopped parsley
1/4 cup vegetable oil
1/4 cup lemon juice, freshly squeezed and strained
salt to taste
freshly ground black pepper to taste

SERVES 6 TO 8.

In a large salad bowl, combine the lettuce, cucumber, green onions, mint, and parsley. In a cup beat the oil and the lemon juice until thoroughly blended. Season with salt and pepper. Pour over the salad and toss.

Eggplant Salad

Simpoog Aghtsa

(THE ILKHANATE)

Most Armenian salads use tomatoes, and this recipe is no exception. Unlike their one-time conquerors, the Mongols, Armenians raise their children on salads and fresh vegetable dishes. Armenian eggplant salad makes an excellent accompaniment to fish, shellfish, or chicken dishes. Russians are notoriously fond of eggplants. This ancient recipe was a favorite in my grandfather's Moscow restaurant.

Salads

> *2 large eggplants*
> *2 medium tomatoes, cut into wedges and seeded*
> *1 medium onion, finely chopped*
> *1/4 cup diced green pepper*
> *1/2 cup peeled and diced cucumber*
> *1/4 cup finely chopped parsley*
> *1 clove garlic, crushed*
> *1/2 cup vegetable oil*
> *3 tablespoons red wine vinegar*
> *salt and freshly ground black pepper, to taste*

SERVES 4 TO 6.

Preheat the oven to 350 degrees F for 10 minutes.

Remove the stems and hulls from the eggplants. Bake for 1 hour. After cooking, allow to cool, then peel off the skin and cut the eggplants open to remove the seeds. Dice and place in a salad bowl.

Add the tomatoes, onion, green pepper, cucumber, and parsley. Then combine the garlic with the oil and stir for 5 minutes, discarding the garlic once its flavor has impregnated the oil. Gently stir in the red wine vinegar and blend thoroughly. Add the salt and pepper, pour over the vegetables. Marinate for 1 hour and chill.

Stir before serving.

Persian Spinach Salad

Borani Esfanaj

(THE ILKHANATE)

When the Mongol storm swept across the Islamic kingdoms to the East under the leadership of Hulegu Khan, the once mighty Persian Empire soon fell to the seemingly invincible invaders. In parts of modern Iran and Iraq where Mongols settled eight centuries ago, Asian faces can be seen in the tea-houses and bazaars. Popular during the blistering summer months, *borani* are cooling Persian salads that make an appealing first course to any meal, simple or elegant. Versions of this recipe have cropped up in Uzbekistan, once part of the Persian Empire and later conquered by Genghis Khan.

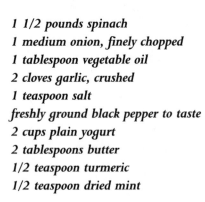

1 1/2 pounds spinach
1 medium onion, finely chopped
1 tablespoon vegetable oil
2 cloves garlic, crushed
1 teaspoon salt
freshly ground black pepper to taste
2 cups plain yogurt
2 tablespoons butter
1/2 teaspoon turmeric
1/2 teaspoon dried mint

SERVES 4 TO 6.

Remove the stalks from the spinach and wash. Drain in a colander and coarsely shred. Using a large, heavy pan, fry the onion in oil until transparent. Add the spinach and stir over medium heat until it wilts. Cook until the moisture evaporates. Stir in the garlic, salt, and pepper. Remove from the heat and allow to cool.

Pour the yogurt in a mixing bow. Stir in the spinach. Toss well. Then melt the butter in a small pan and stir in the turmeric, cooking until the butter turns a golden brown. Add the dried mint. Stir and remove from the heat. Transfer the spinach to a serving bowl and pour the butter mixture over the top.

Lhasa Green Salad
Yaba
(Khanate of the Great Khan)

This dish is a true rarity—a Tibetan salad. Like Mongolia, Tibet is essentially a barren, rugged land with a punishing climate that is not conducive to agriculture. Tibet's arctic winters and frozen peaks make cultivation a nightmare. But the chefs of the Land of Snows have produced a delightful salad recipe, presented in a modified form.

Salads

2 bunches spinach leaves
2 bunches bean sprouts
2 teaspoons honey
3 cloves garlic, finely chopped or crushed
1 teaspoon chopped ginger
1 teaspoon red chili pepper flakes, or to taste
salt to taste
1 cup plain yogurt
2 tablespoons vegetable oil
1/2 teaspoon fenugreek seeds

SERVES 4 TO 6.

Wash the spinach and sprouts and coarsely chop. Place in a large salad bowl. In a cup add the honey, garlic, ginger, red chili pepper, salt, and a 1/4 cup of hot water. Stir thoroughly and pour over the salad. Add the yogurt and mix gently.

In a heavy pan, heat the oil and add the fenugreek seeds, stirring until they turn a dark, rich brown.

Drizzle over the greens and serve.

Bhutanese Chili Pepper Salad

Eze

(KHANATE OF THE GREAT KHAN)

Salads

Perched high in the Himalayas, Bhutan is the world's only Tantric Buddhist kingdom. While Bhutan's early history is unclear, telltale signs of Mongol influence can be found in its religious art. Bhutanese food makes liberal use of hot peppers. The national dish *hemadatsi* is made entirely of chilies served with a cheese sauce. Bhutanese cheeses, ranging from soft and creamy to hard and pungent, find their way into most meals. The nearest or most convenient substitute for *datsi*, which is used in preparing *eze*, is white cheddar or feta. Chilies range from mild to volcanic. This recipe uses a mild variety.

1/2 pound mild Anaheim chilies, stemmed and seeded
1 cup finely chopped white onion
salt to taste
1/2 pound white cheddar or feta, diced into 1/2-inch cubes
3 large tomatoes, sliced into small wedges
1/2 cup red wine vinegar
1/2 cup olive oil

SERVES 4 TO 6.

Cut the chilies into narrow strips and place in a salad bowl. Add white onions, salt, and cheese cubes. Mix thoroughly. Arrange the tomato wedges around the edge of the plate. Mix the red wine vinegar and the olive oil. Pour over the salad.

Serve as a first course or as a side dish.

Ukrainian Cucumber Salad

Miseria

(KHANATE OF THE GOLDEN HORDE)

Although not unique to the Ukrainian kitchen, this salad is widely enjoyed throughout the Russias and Central Asia. Variations of the recipe appear in Turkey, Armenia, and Georgia. It is especially soothing on hot, balmy summer days and makes a delightful accompaniment to fish dishes, which is how it was generally presented in my grandfather's house. The dish would occasionally appear on the menu of his London restaurant and was enjoyed by fellow expatriates.

Salads

6 medium cucumbers, sliced
1 teaspoon salt
1 onion
1/2 cup sour cream or plain yogurt
1 tablespoon sugar or honey
chopped parsley to garnish

SERVES 4 TO 6.

Sprinkle the cucumbers with salt and allow to stand for 10 minutes. Meanwhile, slice the onion. Then mix the sour cream with the sugar. Pour off the liquid from the cucumbers and mix with the sliced onion. Pour the sour cream dressing over the cucumber mixture and chill for 1 hour.

Garnish with parsley.

Georgian Chicken Salad with Herbs

Katmis Mkhali

(KHANATE OF THE GOLDEN HORDE)

This dish is based on a traditional Georgian vegetable puree. Using a combination of chicken, vegetables, herbs, nuts, and even fruit, it is a meal in itself. *Katmis mkhali* makes a delightful light lunch when served with freshly baked, warm bread. While it is doubtful the dish found favor with the khans who ruled over Russia for three centuries, my grandfather had it on good authority that this was one of the favorite dishes of Russia's most ruthless khan—Joseph Stalin.

Salads

>   1 3-pound chicken
>   1 3/4 cups coarsely chopped walnuts
>   2 tablespoons finely ground coriander
>   1/2 teaspoon powdered cardamom
>   1 tablespoon minced garlic
>   2 teaspoons salt
>   5 tablespoons red wine vinegar
>   4 green onions, finely chopped
>   1 cup finely chopped fresh cilantro
>   1/2 cup finely chopped fresh dill
>   1/2 cup finely chopped celery leaves
>   2 cups shredded lettuce
>   1 orange, cut into thin, seeded slices

SERVES 4 TO 6.

Place the chicken in a large pot with 1 quart of water. Bring to a boil, cover, and simmer for 2 hours. Allow the chicken to cool in the stock. Reserve the stock.

Place the walnuts in a mixing bowl and stir in the coriander, cardamom, garlic, salt, and red wine vinegar.

Remove the skin and bones from the chicken and cut the meat into cubes. Combine with the nut mixture. Add 2 cups of the cooking stock. Stir in the green onions, cilantro, dill, and celery. Refrigerate for 3 hours.

Thirty minutes before serving, remove the salad from the refrigerator and place on a bed of shredded lettuce. Garnish with orange slices.

Sauces

Georgian Plum Sauce

Tkemeli

(KHANATE OF THE GOLDEN HORDE)

Sauces

A former Soviet republic, Georgia is best known as the birthplace of Joseph Stalin. As Armenia's neighbor to the north, Georgia was invaded by the Mongols in 1220 and reduced to rubble by the hordes of Timur in 1386 and 1403. Although their contact with the Mongol Empire was one of misfortune, Georgians adopted the Mongolian practice of broiling lamb on skewers, which is called *shashlyk* throughout the former Soviet Union. *Shashlyk* is at its best served with this unique sour plum sauce, a favorite throughout the Russias and Central Asia.

> *1/2 pound red or black plums, pitted*
> *1 clove garlic, minced*
> *3 tablespoons finely chopped cilantro*
> *1/4 teaspoon salt*
> *1/2 teaspoon red chili powder or paprika*
> *3 tablespoons lemon juice, freshly squeezed and strained (about 1 lemon)*

SERVES 4 TO 6.

In a large, heavy pan, bring 2 cups of water to a boil and add the plums. Remove from the heat and allow to sit for 10 minutes. Then return to the heat and bring the water to a gentle boil. Cook uncovered for 15 minutes. Remove the plums and set the liquid aside.

In a blender, combine the plums, garlic, and cilantro. Blend at high speed. Turn off the blender and add 1/4 cup of the reserved water. Blend for a few minutes, then stop to add the remaining water. Continue to blend until the mixture is thick and creamy.

Transfer the mixture to a heavy saucepan and stir in the salt and chili powder. Bring to a boil, remove from the heat and stir in the lemon juice. Allow the sauce to cool. Store in a clean glass jar and refrigerate until ready to use. Warm in a heavy saucepan, but do not allow to boil.

Pour over Georgian *shashlyk* (page 98) and serve on a bed of rice.

Herb and Walnut Sauce
Tarator
(THE ILKHANATE)

An unusual sauce of Turkish origin, *tarator* is generally served over fish or vegetables. Many Armenians enjoy *tarator* over fried mussels or oysters. The use of walnuts has all but disappeared in present-day Mongolia, but they were once imported and held in high esteem.

Sauces

>*2 slices white bread*
>*1/2 cup walnut halves*
>*1 clove garlic, peeled and crushed*
>*1/2 cup vegetable oil or walnut oil*
>*1 tablespoon wine vinegar*
>*1 teaspoon red chili pepper flakes or cayenne*
>*3 teaspoons paprika*
>*salt to taste*

SERVES 4 TO 6.

Soak the bread in water for 10 minutes, trim off the crusts then squeeze dry. Pulverize the walnuts in a blender. Add the garlic and continue to blend. Then add the bread and blend for 15 seconds. Add the oil, vinegar, red pepper flakes, paprika, and salt. Blend on a slow setting until the mixture becomes thick, creamy,and smooth. Store in a clean glass jar and refrigerate. *Tarator* complements fried fish, chicken, seafood, beans, cauliflower, and eggplant.

Garlic Yogurt Sauce

Sikhdorov Madzoon

(THE ILKHANATE)

Yogurt has been used in Mongolia and throughout the Middle East since recorded history. Mongolian yogurt is usually made from the milk of yaks, which is enough to clog your arteries for the next decade. This modified recipe can be used to enhance the flavor of vegetable and lamb dishes. In fact, it is sometimes used to marinate lamb for kabobs.

Sauces

> *1 cup plain yogurt*
> *1 to 2 cloves garlic, peeled*
> *1/4 teaspoon salt*
> *1/2 teaspoon dried and crushed mint leaves*
> *black pepper to taste*

SERVES 4 TO 6.

Place the yogurt in a mixing bowl. Pound the garlic with the salt, mint, and pepper. Stir the mixture into the yogurt and refrigerate for 2 hours before serving, or use as a marinade for lamb or beef.

Blackberry Sauce
Malvali
(Khanate of the Golden Horde)

This unusual sauce uses a combination of sweet, sour, and hot flavors. Most often it is used on roast chicken, giving it a rich red color. It is equally good on roast duck, partridge, game hens, or venison. For house specials and parties, my grandfather took boundless pride in his presentation of wild duck with *makvali*. It always brought smiles to his guests' faces—and mine.

Sauces

> *2 cups fresh blackberries (use frozen or canned*
> *when out of season)*
> *1 teaspoon crushed garlic*
> *1/3 teaspoon salt*
> *1 teaspoon crushed red chili pepper, or to taste*
> *2 tablespoons finely chopped fresh dill*
> *2 tablespoons finely chopped fresh cilantro*
> *2 teaspoons lemon juice, freshly squeezed and strained*

SERVES 4 TO 6.

Place the blackberries in a blender and puree. Add the garlic, salt, and chili pepper. Blend for 30 seconds. Warm gently. Remove to a serving dish and stir in the chopped herbs and lemon juice.

Tartar Sauce

Tatar 'ka Pidlyva

(KHANATE OF THE GREAT KHAN)

This sauce was introduced into the Ukraine by bands of Tatar Mongols, who eventually settled and integrated into Ukrainian society. Unlike the Americanized version, genuine tartar sauce is not restricted to fish but is often served with roasts and smoked meats. This version is centuries old and is far tastier than commercial Westernized versions.

Sauces

6 egg yolks, cooked
2 tablespoons vegetable oil
1 teaspoon prepared mustard
1 tablespoon vinegar
1 tablespoon horseradish sauce
2 tablespoons sour cream or plain yogurt
1 teaspoon sugar
2 tablespoons chopped dill pickles

SERVES 4 TO 6.

In a mixing bowl, mash the egg yolks. Stir in the remaining ingredients. Store in a tightly covered glass jar and refrigerate.

Tibetan Hot Sauce

Sipen Mardur

(KHANATE OF THE GREAT KHAN)

Unlike many fiery Tibetan hot sauces, this preparation is cooled by the use of yogurt. *Sipen mardur* is surprisingly versatile and can be served to complement meat and chicken dishes or to lend flavor, color, and texture to rice.

Sauces

1 medium tomato
3 teaspoons red chili pepper flakes, or to taste
1 cup plain yogurt
3 cloves garlic, finely minced
salt to taste
1 teaspoon minced ginger
1/2 cup finely chopped cilantro
1 tablespoon paprika

SERVES 4 TO 6.

Boil the tomato for 2 minutes then place in a blender along with the red pepper flakes and yogurt. Add the garlic, salt, and ginger. Blend for 2 minutes. Pour into a mixing bowl. Add the cilantro and paprika. Cover with plastic wrap and chill before using.

Breads

Flat Onion Bread

Non

(CHAGHADAI KHANATE)

This unusual dish comes from one the culturally richest areas of Central Asia, Uzbekistan. Invaded by Genghis Khan in the thirteenth century, Uzbeks are a people of Turkic, Iranian, and Mongolian stock. The ancient cities of Samarkand and Bukhara are famous for their carpets, mosques, and distinctive cuisine. No self-respecting Uzbek family would consider serving a meal without including *non*, a tasty, delicate onion bread.

Breads

> *6 tablespoons butter*
> *1 1/2 cups finely chopped onions*
> *3/4 cup lukewarm water*
> *1 teaspoon salt*
> *2 1/2 to 3 cups all-purpose flour*

SERVES 4 TO 6.

Using high heat, melt 1 tablespoon of butter in a large, heavy pan. Stir in the onions and reduce the heat to low. Cook for 5 minutes, stirring occasionally until the onions are soft but not brown. Remove the onions from the heat and place them in a bowl to cool to room temperature.

Melt the remaining 5 tablespoons butter then pour it into a large bowl. Add the lukewarm water. Then stir in the onions, salt, and 1/2 cup of the flour at a time until the dough does not stick to your fingers. Form the dough into a ball and divide it into 15 equal parts. Using the palm of your hand, shape each piece into a 2-inch ball. Dab a little flour on a rolling pin and roll the balls of dough into circles 8 inches in diameter. Set the dough aside.

Place a large, heavy ungreased pan over high heat until a drop of water placed on the surface evaporates almost immediately. Place one round of dough in the pan and cook for

Imperial Mongolian Cooking

3 to 4 minutes on each side.

Place the cooked bread on a cooling rack, then cook the remaining dough rounds. The bread should be stored in a porous container. If the bread loses its crisp texture, heat it in the oven at 250 degrees F for 5 to 10 minutes.

Tibetan Fried Bread

Kapse

(KHANATE OF THE GREAT KHAN)

In the United States, fried bread is generally associated with Native Americans. It is also a great favorite of Tibetans, who rely heavily on grains, particularly barley for sustenance. Wheat is only grown in small quantities in Tibet's warmer valleys. Here is another Buddhist recipe my grandfather culled from the philandering Dorje: lama, chef, royal incubus, soldier, and family friend.

Breads

> *2 cups whole-wheat flour*
> *2 cups all-purpose flour*
> *2 teaspoons baking powder*
> *2 cups nonfat milk*
> *3 teaspoons sugar*
> *4 cups vegetable oil*

SERVES 4 TO 6.

In a large plastic mixing bowl combine the flours and the baking powder. Mix the milk and sugar in another bowl until the sugar is dissolved. Then add the milk mixture to the flour and knead until it is stiff. Cut the stiff dough into pieces 2 inches long and 3 to 4 inches wide. Roll into balls and then flatten them with a rolling pin.

Heat the oil in a deep pan until it becomes very hot. Drop in one piece of bread at a time and cook until it is lightly browned. Place on a paper towel to absorb the excess oil and serve plain or with honey.

Steamed Bread, Tibetan Style

Trimomo

(Khanate of the Great Khan)

Tibetans love bread in all forms. *Trimomo* is served with sauces or as an accompaniment to curry. Originally adapted from the Chinese, the recipe was passed along to the Mongols who delight in filling the dough with spiced ground meat and call the dish *buuz*. Either preparation is colorful, tasty, and exotic.

Breads

> *2 teaspoons yeast*
> *2 teaspoons baking soda*
> *1 cup lukewarm water*
> *3 cups whole-wheat flour*
> *3 cups all-purpose flour*
> *2 cups vegetable oil*
> *3 teaspoons turmeric*

Serves 4 to 6.

Add the yeast and baking soda to the lukewarm water, stirring until completely dissolved. Combine the flours in a mixing bowl and add 1 cup of the mixture to the water, stirring well. Allow the mixture to sit for 2 to 3 hours in a warm, draft-free place. Add the remaining flour and knead into a dough that is stiff but still flexible. Divide the dough into two equal portions and roll until it is a flat round 1/8 inch thick. Mix the oil and the turmeric. Lightly brush the dough with the mixture.

Cut the dough into 2-inch sections and roll each piece into a ball. Press the bottom against a wooden board dusted with flour. Make sure the bottom is flat and the top remains rounded.

Brush a steamer with a little butter. Put the dough into it in rows, allowing a little space between each piece so that they do not touch.

Steam over high heat for 20 minutes.

Afghan Wholegrain Bread

Naun

(The Ilkhanate)

Breads

Afghanistan was plundered by Genghis Khan and ruled over by his successors. Its strongest link with the Mongol Empire began with Babar, a direct decedent of Genghis Khan, an Afghanistani overlord who founded the Moghul Empire in India. While there are many variations of this recipe throughout Central Asia, Afghani *naun* is one the tastiest and can be prepared quickly and easily.

> *1 package active dry yeast*
> *2 cups warm water*
> *3 cups wholegrain flour*
> *2 cups all-purpose flour*
> *1 1/2 teaspoons salt*
> *1/3 cup olive oil*

SERVES 15.

Dissolve the yeast in 1/4 cup of warm water. Sift the flours and salt in a mixing bowl, removing any flakes left after sifting. Add the remaining 3/4 cup warm water to the yeast mixture, then pour into the middle of the flour mixture. Stir only a little flour into the liquid to thicken.

Cover the bowl and leave in a warm, draft-free place for 10 minutes or until the mixture becomes frothy. Slowly add the remainder of the flour and beat for 20 minutes. Knead and cover the bowl. Leave in a warm place until it rises to twice its original size. This can take from 30 minutes to an hour.

Preheat the oven to 425 degrees F for 10 minutes. Lightly oil your hands and divide the dough into eight equal portions, rolling them into balls. Take a dough ball and work it into a pear shape about 1/2 inch thick on a lightly oiled wooden board. Set the dough on a baking sheet and cover with a clean cloth for 15 minutes. After dipping your finger in the oil make 3 parallel grooves in each dough loaf by pressing your finger along the sides. The grooves should begin about 3/4 of an inch before the edges of the dough.

Pop the dough into the center of the oven and bake for 15 minutes, or until the loaves are lightly brown. Remove from the oven, wrap in cloth and serve.

Sesame Rolls
Shoushayov Gatah
(THE ILKHANATE)

Breads

Armenian lore proclaims that their country was founded by Haig, a descendent of Noah. Yet few people have endured more hardships than the Armenians. Invaded by the notoriously brutal Assyrians, Medes, and ancient Persians, the country was conquered by the Mongols in the thirteenth century and incorporated into the Empire. While Armenian cookery influenced the Mongols, few Armenian dishes are actually of Mongol or Tatar origin. *Shoushayov gatah* is a purely Armenian creation.

3/4 cake compressed yeast
1/3 cup lukewarm water
4 cups sifted all-purpose flour
3 eggs
1/2 teaspoon turmeric
1/2 cup butter, melted
1/2 cup condensed milk
1/2 cup sugar
1 to 2 tablespoons sesame seeds

SERVES 4 TO 6.

Dissolve the yeast in the lukewarm water. Place the flour in a large bowl, making a well in the center. Place the yeast mixture, 2 of the eggs, turmeric, melted butter, milk, and sugar in the well. Stir the ingredients and blend into the flour. Sprinkle a little flour on a wooden cutting board and knead the flour mixture until it turns into a smooth dough. Shape it into a ball and place it in a clean bowl, covering with a cloth. Let it sit in a warm, draft-free place for 3 hours until the dough doubles in size.

Compress the dough. Sprinkle your hands with a little flour and break off small portions of dough, rolling them into ropes 12 inches long and 1/2 inch thick. Wind each rope to form a snail-like coil. Place the rolls on a baking sheet allowing 2 inches between each roll.

Brush the tops with the remaining beaten egg and sprinkle with sesame seeds. Cover with a cloth and let the dough rise in a warm place for 2 hours.

Preheat the oven to 375 degrees F for 10 minutes. Bake for 15 to 20 minutes until the rolls are golden brown.

Bean Bread

Lobiani

(KHANATE OF THE GOLDEN HORDE)

The breads of Georgia are unique. As an agricultural society, Georgians placed great emphasis on the growing and utilization of grain—quite the opposite of their Mongol conquers, nomads who saw no sense in being tied to one piece of land year-round. While the Mongols eventually learned the art of bread-making from the Russians, they never reached the creative level of the Georgians.

Breads

DOUGH:
> *5 tablespoons butter or margarine, softened*
> *1 egg*
> *1 cup sour cream*
> *5 cups plain flour*
> *2 teaspoons baking soda*

FILLING:
> *1/2 pound dried kidney beans, soaked overnight in 6 cups water*
> *2 medium onions, diced*
> *1/3 cup vegetable oil*
> *1/2 teaspoon powdered coriander*
> *1 teaspoon salt*
> *black pepper to taste*
> *1/2 egg yolk, beaten*

SERVES 8 TO 10.

In a large mixing bowl, soften the butter and beat in the egg and sour cream. Knead in the flour to make a soft dough.

On a floured wooden board, roll out the dough into a large rectangle, about 8 inches by 10 inches. Sprinkle with 1/4 teaspoon of baking soda, then fold the dough in half. Roll out into another rectangle and sprinkle with 1/4 teaspoon of baking soda. Fold the dough again and repeat the sprinkling and rolling out until all the baking soda has been used.

Place the dough in a lightly floured bowl, cover, and leave to rise in a warm, draft-free area until it doubles in size.

While the dough is rising, drain the beans. Place them in a pan and cover them with fresh water. Bring the water to a boil, reduce to simmer and cook for 1 hour. Drain the beans and mash them until they are smooth.

Sauté the onions in oil until they are transparent and soft. Stir into the mashed beans. Add the coriander, salt, and pepper.

Preheat the oven to 425 degrees F for 10 minutes. Roll out the dough on a lightly floured baking sheet until it is 1 1/2-inches thick. Spread the bean mixture over half the dough. Fold the uncovered half and seal by forcing the lower edges over the top of the dough, thereby making a rim. Brush the bread with the beaten egg yolk.

Bake for 40 minutes or until golden brown. Serve warm.

Honey Bread
Madivnyk
(KHANATE OF THE GOLDEN HORDE)

This bread is prized for its strong, rich flavor. Like Georgians, Ukrainians have raised the craft of baking to an art form. *Madivnyk* is usually reserved for celebrations such as Christmas. It is often baked ahead of time and frozen until the holidays arrive. My grandfather always featured it on the menu around Christmas.

Breads

> *14 ounces honey*
> *8 eggs*
> *6 tablespoons butter*
> *1 1/2 cups sugar*
> *6 1/2 cups of plain flour*
> *2 teaspoons baking powder*
> *1 teaspoons baking soda*
> *2 teaspoons ground cinnamon*
> *zest and juice of 1 orange*
> *1 cup strong black coffee, unsweetened*
> *1 cup sour cream*
> *1 cup chopped walnuts*

SERVES 12.

Preheat the oven to 325 degrees F for 10 minutes prior to baking.

In a heavy saucepan, heat the honey until it boils and remove from the stove. Let it cool. Meanwhile, separate the eggs. In a large mixing bowl, beat the yolks with the butter until fluffy. Stir in the honey once it has cooled and beat. Add the sugar and blend thoroughly.

Imperial Mongolian Cooking

Sift the flour, baking powder, baking soda, and cinnamon. Add the mixture to the honey butter. Then stir in the orange juice and zest, coffee, and sour cream. Mix thoroughly, then whip the egg whites until stiff and fold a little into the flour. Stir well and repeat the process. Finally, stir in the walnuts.

Butter and lightly flour 2 loaf pans, and fill with the batter. Bake for 1 hour. Set aside and allow to cool. Serve at room temperature. Alternatively, allow to cool, wrap in aluminum foil, and freeze until read to use.

Poultry
& Game

Stewed Rabbit or Hare

Tolah

(KHANATE OF THE GREAT KHAN)

With the curious exception of marmots, Mongolians scorn the eating of rodents, including rabbits and hares. This was not always so. Before state banquets, high officials in the Mongol court would dispatch hunters to bring in deer and rabbits, sometimes for offerings to the spirit deities or as food. The season for rabbits in Central Asia is from September to March.

This ancient dish is sometimes served in Inner Mongolia. During the fall of 1904 when my grandfather was stationed in Mongolia, a shipment of rations failed to arrive on time. Dorje taught him to hunt for hares and how to prepare them according to a recipe favored by Khubilai Khan.

6 pounds rabbit, skinned and cut into small pieces
juice of 1 lemon, freshly squeezed and strained
1/2 cup soy sauce
3 tablespoons rice wine
1 tablespoon minced ginger
3 tablespoons paprika
1 white onion, quartered
1 tablespoon sugar
2 carrots, julienned

SERVES 6.

Wash the rabbit and soak in salted water with the lemon juice for 3 hours. Rinse and place it a heavy cooking pot. Cover with 3 cups of fresh water and bring to a boil. Add the soy sauce, wine, ginger, paprika, and onion. Reduce the heat, cover and simmer for 2 hours. Then stir in the sugar and carrots. Cover tightly and simmer for an additional hour or until tender.

Roasted Rabbit or Hare

Khorovdz Nabasdag

(THE ILKHANATE)

Armenians will often barbecue rabbit or hare over an open fire. However, this traditional recipe requires the rabbit to be slowly roasted in an oven, which produces a delicate and tender dish. If using hare, it should be hung for a few days or marinated overnight to tenderize.

6 pounds rabbit or hare, cut into small pieces
1/2 cup butter, melted, or olive oil
salt to taste
black pepper to taste
2 teaspoons garlic juice
2 tablespoons paprika
2 tablespoons red wine
3 tablespoons lemon juice, freshly squeezed and strained (about 1 lemon)
2 apples, sautéed

SERVES 6 TO 8.

Preheat the oven to 425 degrees F for 10 minutes before cooking.

Dry the rabbit using paper towels. Brush the butter on the bottom and sides of an oven dish. Place the rabbit in the dish and cook for 15 minutes. Remove from the oven and reduce heat the 325 degrees F. Blend the remaining butter with the salt, pepper, garlic juice, paprika, and wine. Return to the oven cook for 1 hour, basting with juices and spice mixture every 15 minutes.

During the last 15 minutes of cooking, brush the rabbit with the lemon juice. When the meat is done, place it under the broiler for 5 minutes.

Place on a platter and serve with a rice dish. Garnish with slices of sautéed apple.

Yuan Venison

Bouch

(KHANATE OF THE GREAT KHAN)

The Mongol court of Khubilai Khan often produced sumptuous meals. Among the many dishes enjoyed by nobles and visiting dignitaries was venison. Today among the Mongols of Tuva, venison is often served, particularly as a spicy noodle soup flavored with juniper and wild onions.

1/4 cup vegetable oil
2 pounds venison, sliced paper thin
1 teaspoon salt, or to taste
1/2 teaspoon finely ground black pepper
2 teaspoons finely grated ginger
2 cups dried shiitake mushrooms, soaked, stemmed, and finely sliced
unpeeled sugar cane, cut into 4 small pieces
1 cup vegetable stock
1 tablespoon sherry
2 cups finely sliced water chestnuts

SERVES 4 TO 6.

In a wok or heavy saucepan, heat the oil and add the venison, stirring constantly. Stir in the salt, pepper, and ginger. Then stir in the mushrooms and sugar cane. Stir-fry for 5 minutes.

Pour in the stock and bring to a boil. Put the meat and vegetable mixture in a larger steamer. Sprinkle with sherry and steam for 1 3/4 hours. Add the water chestnuts, steam for 15 minutes, and serve.

Pheasant in Wine
Kiniov Pasean
(THE ILKHANATE)

Although simple to prepare, this is one of most delectable Armenian dishes. It was also eaten in a different preparation in Mongolia as *khujar* or wild dove. If pheasant is not available, the dish works well with a medium capon. But nothing rivals the delicate taste and subtle texture of pheasant. A meal fit for a khan.

Poultry & Game

1 large pheasant
salt to taste
1/2 cup plus 2 teaspoons butter
3 carrots, julienned
1 1/2 cups dry white wine
2 teaspoons all-purpose flour
4 potatoes, thinly sliced
2 cups vegetable oil
2 tablespoons finely chopped parsley

SERVES 4 TO 6.

Wipe the pheasant inside and out with paper towels until completely dry. Sprinkle with salt. Melt 1/2 cup butter in a heavy, ovenproof casserole and fry until the pheasant turns an even golden brown. Add the carrots. Pour the wine over the pheasant and cover. Simmer over low heat for 45 minutes, adding a little stock if the bird begins to dry out.

Cut into serving portions. Strain off the juices and wine from the pan. Pour into a saucepan. Melt the remaining 2 teaspoons of butter and stir in the flour. Reduce heat and stir in the wine and pan juices. Stir until it thickens and pour over the pheasant. Fry the potatoes in the vegetable oil until golden brown.

Serve the pheasant with the fried potatoes. Garnish with parsley.

Grilled Partridges

Khujar

(KHANATE OF THE GREAT KHAN)

Dating from the thirteenth century, this recipe originally called for wild dove. Unlike Westerners, Mongolians do not regard the dove as a symbol of peace and have no compunction in serving them roasted to honored guests. I have substituted partridges, which can usually be ordered through one's local butcher. Feel free to use game hens instead, which are readily available in most supermarkets, allowing 1 bird for each guest.

Poultry
& Game

> *4 partridges*
> *salt to taste*
> *1/2 cup butter*
> *juice of 1 lemon, freshly squeezed and strained*
> *1/2 teaspoon finely ground ginger*
> *1/8 teaspoon five-spice powder*
> *1/2 cup finely chopped green onions*
> *medium bunch red seedless grapes*
>
> **Serves 4.**

Dry the partridges with paper towels. Sprinkle with salt. Melt the butter and stir in the lemon juice, ginger, and five-spice powder.

Brush the birds with the spiced butter mixture and grill over hot coals, turning until browned on all sides. Baste frequently.

Arrange on individual dishes and sprinkle with the green onions. Serve with rice and a vegetable side dish.

Garnish with red grapes.

Mongolian Quail or Partridge

Yatoe

(KHANATE OF THE GREAT KHAN)

Yatoe is an uncommon dish among Mongols who prefer the richness of lamb to the delicate flavors of quail and partridge. It is believed that the rulers of the Khanate of the Great Khan, which encompassed both Mongolia and most of what is present-day China, were introduced to the dish by Chinese chefs. During Dorje's service to the last khan, this was one of the favorite dishes of his consort.

Poultry
& Game

> 1/3 cup oil
> 6 quails or four partridges, cut into small pieces
> 2 cups sliced water chestnuts
> 2 cups sliced mushrooms
> 1 teaspoon grated ginger
> 1 1/4 cups chicken or vegetable stock
> 2 teaspoons sherry or rice wine
> 2 tablespoons cornstarch
> 2 to 3 tablespoons mushroom soy sauce
> 1 teaspoon salt
> 1 head lettuce, shredded
> 2 cups finely chopped green onions

SERVES 4.

Heat the oil in a wok. Stir-fry the quails until brown. Stir in the water chestnuts, mushrooms, and ginger. Blend well. Then stir in the stock mixed with the sherry. Reduce the heat, cover, and cook for 15 minutes.

Blend the cornstarch, soy sauce, salt, and 1/2 cup water. Stir into the wok and raise the temperature slightly. Keep stirring until the mixture thickens.

Place the quails on top of shredded lettuce and sprinkle with the green onions.

Serve with rice, buns, and sliced bell peppers, carrots, and radishes.

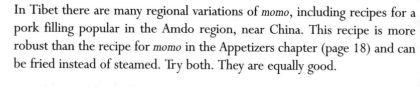

Spicy Steamed Chicken Dumplings
Momo (Chicken)
(KHANATE OF THE GREAT KHAN)

In Tibet there are many regional variations of *momo*, including recipes for a pork filling popular in the Amdo region, near China. This recipe is more robust than the recipe for *momo* in the Appetizers chapter (page 18) and can be fried instead of steamed. Try both. They are equally good.

FILLING:

> 1/3 cup hot water
> 2 tablespoons mushroom soy sauce
> 1 tablespoon crushed garlic
> 1 teaspoon finely grated ginger
> 2 to 3 tablespoons finely chopped cilantro
> salt and black pepper, to taste
> 4 tablespoons rice wine or dry sherry
> chili oil to taste
> 1/2 teaspoon finely ground cumin
> 1/2 teaspoon finely ground nutmeg
> 1/2 cup minced mushrooms
> 1/2 cup finely chopped spinach
> 1 1/2 pounds ground chicken

DOUGH:

> 3 cups all-purpose flour
> 3 cups whole-wheat flour
> 1 teaspoon baking soda

SERVES 6 TO 8.

In a large nonmetal mixing bowl, blend the hot water with the soy sauce, garlic, ginger, cilantro, salt, pepper, wine, chili oil, cumin, nutmeg, mushrooms, and spinach. Add the ground chicken and mix thoroughly.

Using a separate mixing bowl, combine the flours and baking soda. Add enough water to make a stiff dough. Break off a small chunk of dough and roll into a 3/4-inch ball. Flatten it slightly and dust with flour. Push a rolling pin across the dough, then push the dough from the edge to the middle. Do the same from the opposite side until the dough becomes a 4-inch circle that is slightly thicker in the middle.

Put a teaspoon of filling in the center of the dough. Fold into a half-moon shape. Firmly pinch the edges together. Then bend the *momo* holding your thumb in the middle and pinch the right edge to reseal at the bend.

Brush the bottom and sides of a steamer with vegetable oil. Place the *momo* in the steamer so that they neither touch each other nor the sides of the steamer. This will prevent them from sticking. Bring the water in the steamer (about 6 to 9 cups, depending on its size) to a rolling boil. Cover tightly and cook for 10 minutes.

Serve with *sipen mardur* hot sauce (page 64) and *dresil* saffron rice (page 165).

Chicken-Filled Buns

Bao

(KHANATE OF THE GREAT KHAN)

Bao is the Tibetan version of Mongolian *buuz*, which are usually filled with lamb or mutton. Like *momo*, Tibetan buns are steamed and can be made with a variety of fillings. This version was among my grandfather's favorites, which he adapted from the Mongolia days of his youth. The dish is delightfully subtle, much more so than the traditional Mongolian version, which tends to be on the heavy side.

FILLING:
> 1/4 cup vegetable oil
> 1/2 cup finely chopped onions
> 1 1/2 pounds ground chicken
> 1/2 cup finely chopped spinach or bok choy
> 1/2 cup chopped mushrooms
> 1 tablespoon minced garlic
> 1 teaspoon finely grated ginger
> 2 tablespoons mushroom soy sauce
> 1/2 teaspoon sesame oil
> chili oil to taste

DOUGH:
> 1/2 cup whole milk
> 1/2 tablespoon yeast
> 2 tablespoons honey
> 1 tablespoon shortening
> 2 cups unbleached flour, sifted

Serves 6 to 8.

In a heavy saucepan, heat a few tablespoons of oil and brown the onions. Remove from the heat and allow to cool. Using a large mixing bowl, blend the chicken with the spinach, mushrooms, onions, garlic, ginger, and soy sauce. Stir in the chili and sesame oils and mix thoroughly.

In a heavy pan, scald the milk and remove from the heat. Cool until luke-warm. Stir in the yeast and the honey. Add the shortening to the flour. When the milk is bubbly, stir it into the flour. Then knead until stiff. Cover and allow the dough to rise until it doubles in size, which should take an hour. Knead the dough and cover. Let it rise until it again doubles its previous size.

Punch down the dough and knead for 1 minute. Break off a piece of dough about 3/4 inch in diameter, roll it into a ball and flatten slightly on a floured wooden board. Roll the dough into a circle and place a tablespoon of filling in the center. Stretching the dough, push the edges up toward the center. When they meet, firmly pinch the dough together.

Place in a lightly oiled steamer. Bring the water to a rolling boil, cover and steam for 20 minutes.

Serve with rice and *sipen mardur* hot sauce (page 64).

Orange Chicken Rice Pilaf
Zarda Palau
(The Ilkhanate)

Traditionally, Afghanistanis prepare this dish with sugar—lots of it. This version cuts the sweetness by adding a little lemon juice and replacing the sugar with a small amount of honey, which makes the dish far more delicate and interesting. The art of preparing a good *zarda palau* takes a little patience and practice to acquire, but the results well justify the effort.

Poultry
& Game

> *rind of 2 oranges, thinly peeled*
> *1/4 cup honey*
> *juice of 1/2 lemon, freshly squeezed and strained*
> *1/4 cup vegetable oil*
> *1/2 cup slivered almonds*
> *2 pounds boneless, skinless chicken breasts*
> *1/2 teaspoons salt, or to taste*
> *1/4 teaspoon freshly ground black pepper*
> *1 red onion, finely chopped*
> *1 cup chicken stock*
> *2 cups long-grain white rice*
> *1/2 teaspoon turmeric*
> *1/4 cup pistachio nuts, blanched*
> *1/2 tablespoon paprika*

SERVES 6 TO 8.

Preheat the oven to 300 degrees F for 10 minutes before cooking.

Cut the orange peel into 1-inch strips. Boil in 2 cups of water for 5 minutes, then drain and rinse. In a separate saucepan, dissolve the honey in 1 cup of water. Turn the heat to medium and stir in the lemon juice. Bring to a boil then reduce the heat, cooking for 5 minutes. Remove from the heat and set aside.

In a large saucepan, heat 1 tablespoon of the oil. Stir in the almonds and cook until golden brown. Remove from the pan and set aside. Add the remaining 3 tablespoons oil and brown the chicken. Remove the chicken and season with 1/2 teaspoon of salt and the pepper. Add the onion to the saucepan and cook until golden brown. Stir in the chicken stock. When hot, add the chicken breasts. Cover and simmer for 20 minutes.

Wash the rice until all the starch is removed and the rinse water runs clear. In a large pot, bring 8 cups of water to a boil and add the rice and a teaspoon of salt. Boil for 8 minutes and drain. Put the rice into a large mixing bowl and pour the honey and lemon syrup over the top. Stir in the turmeric. Mix thoroughly and spread half the rice onto a lightly oiled casserole dish.

Arrange the chicken breasts on top of the rice. Add half the stock. Sprinkle with half the onions, orange peel, and almonds. Spread the remaining rice on top and add the rest of the stock. Cover with the remaining onions, orange peel, almonds, and pistachios. Cover tightly.

Bake for 45 minutes. When the dish is cooked, arrange the top layer of rice around the edge of a serving platter. Put the bottom layer of rice in the center and top with the chicken.

Sprinkle with paprika and serve.

Yogurt Chicken

Zaporozhste

(KHANATE OF THE GOLDEN HORDE)

A light and delicate traditional Ukrainian meal, *zaporozhste* is easy to prepare yet elegant enough to be served at any dinner party. After my grandfather's London restaurant succumbed to fire, he spent his remaining years as a caterer to Russian expatriates. This was one of his most successful dishes, one he also regularly prepared for us.

Poultry
& Game

> *2 cups plain yogurt*
> *2 tablespoons freshly squeezed lemon juice, strained (about 1 lemon)*
> *1 teaspoon dried mustard*
> *2 teaspoons paprika*
> *1 teaspoon finely chopped fresh dill*
> *1 tablespoon crushed garlic*
> *1/2 teaspoon thyme*
> *salt and pepper, to taste*
> *6 boneless, skinless chicken breasts*
> *2 cups unseasoned bread crumbs*

SERVES 6.

Preheat the oven to 350 degrees F 10 minutes before baking.

Place the yogurt in a mixing bowl and stir in the lemon juice, mustard, paprika, dill, garlic, thyme, and salt and pepper. Dip the chicken in the yogurt then place in a separate bowl filled with bread crumbs, making sure that both sides are well coated. Place in a baking dish. Cook for 50 minutes, or until the chicken breasts are golden brown.

Serve with plain rice and a side salad.

Duck With Walnuts

Ikhvis Chakohkhbili

(KHANATE OF THE GOLDEN HORDE)

Although often made with chicken, this dish is best when duck is used. Prized at Xanadu, the court of Khubilai Khan, duck has fallen into disfavor with modern Mongolians. However, it is widely enjoyed in other parts of their former empire, especially in China and the Russias. While Peking Duck has become something of a culinary cliché, this Georgian preparation is similar to *fasinjan*, the version from Persia. Flavorful and robust, it is even better when reheated the second day.

Poultry & Game

1 large duck, jointed and cut into 12 pieces
1 large onion, finely chopped
6 tomatoes, chopped
1 tablespoon all-purpose flour
1 tablespoon finely chopped garlic
1/2 teaspoon ground coriander
1/4 teaspoon turmeric
1/2 teaspoon salt, or to taste
black pepper to taste
1/2 cup finely chopped cilantro
2 tablespoons red wine vinegar
1/4 cup lemon juice, freshly squeezed and strained (about 1 1/2 lemons)
1 cup ground walnuts
1 tablespoon cornmeal

SERVES 4.

Preheat the oven to 350 degrees F for 10 minutes before cooking.

Place the duck in a large casserole dish, cover, and cook for 1 hour. Remove the duck from the dish and drain off the fat. Return the duck to the casserole and add the onion. Cover and roast for an additional 30 minutes.

-CONTINUED-

Remove from the heat and cover with a layer of chopped tomatoes. Cover and cook for another 30 minutes.

In a nonmetal mixing bowl, blend the flour, garlic, coriander, turmeric, salt, pepper, cilantro, vinegar, and lemon juice. Remove the duck from the oven and transfer to the bowl along with the cooked onions and tomatoes. Cover tightly.

Stir 1 1/2 cups of the cooking liquid from the casserole into the nuts and cornmeal. Mix well. Return the duck and vegetables to the casserole and cover with the sauce. Bake for 15 minutes.

Serve with rice and warm bread.

Lamb

Skewered Lamb

Shashlyk

No other dish captures the culinary spirit of the former USSR more than *shashlyk*. A favorite throughout Central Asia, especially in the jeweled cities of Samarkand and Bukhara, the Georgian version presented here was a great success at my grandfather's restaurant, beloved by Londoners and Russian expatriates alike. In Georgia, grilled meat falls into two categories: *mtswadi*, made from fresh, unmarinated meat; and *basturma*, made from marinated meat. The marinade is carried around by the hunters until they can make a kill. *Shashlyk* is the undisputed khan of *basturma*.

Lamb

1 large onion, peeled and grated
juice of 1 lemon, freshly squeezed and strained
2 cloves garlic, finely chopped
1 tablespoon olive oil
1 teaspoon salt
1/4 teaspoon finely ground black pepper
2 pounds leg of lamb, trimmed of fat and cut into 1-inch cubes
2 medium red onions, cut into 1/4-inch chunks
2 medium tomatoes, each cut into 8 wedges
1 lemon, quartered
3/4 cup coarsely chopped green onions

SERVES 4 TO 6.

Blend the grated onion, lemon juice, garlic, oil, salt, and pepper in a large mixing bowl. Add the lamb, cover, and marinate for 3 hours, turning every 30 minutes.

Place the marinated cubes on long skewers, alternating chunks of lamb with cubes of red onion. Broil over hot coals, turning frequently until the lamb is done and the onions are brown, 15 to 20 minutes.

Slide the lamb and onion mixture off the skewers and serve over a bed of rice. Garnish with tomatoes and lemon quarters.

Serve with *tkemeli* plum sauce (page 58). Sprinkle generously with green onions.

Mongolian Barbecued Lamb
Shorlog
(KHANATE OF THE GREAT KHAN)

Lamb

If any one meal could be identified as Mongolia's national dish, this is it. Said to have been a favorite of the last khan, the recipe has been adapted from the one handed down by my grandfather. There are many regional variations of *shorlog*, this one chosen since it calls for the lamb to be cooked over coals in keeping with the American tradition of barbecuing. In Central Asia, the entire carcass is roasted on a large spit. A simple dish, *shorlog* is not frequently served in Mongolia as the harsh winters force most families to prepare food indoors.

> *1 large, boneless leg of lamb*
> *salt to taste*
> *freshly ground black pepper*
> *3 tablespoons finely crushed garlic*
> *1 tablespoon finely grated ginger*
> *3 tablespoons paprika*
> *1/4 cup vegetable oil*
> *2 teaspoons sesame oil*
> *1/3 cup sliced almonds*
> *1/3 cup sesame seeds*
> *3/4 cup finely chopped cilantro*

SERVES 8 TO 10.

Rub the lamb with salt and pepper. Mix the garlic, ginger, and paprika with the oils, blending thoroughly. With a sharp knife, make series of fine slits in the lamb. Brush the oil and spice mixture over the meat. Allow to marinate for at least 2 hours before cooking. Turn frequently and baste while marinating.

Make sure the coals are white hot. Place the lamb on a spit and begin cooking over the hot coals, turning frequently and basting evenly every 10 minutes. When the meat is cooked evenly, cut it into thin slices. Sprinkle with sliced almonds, sesame seeds, and chopped cilantro.

Imperial Mongolian Cooking

Rice Pilaf With Lamb and Vegetables
Uzbek Palov
(Chaghadai Khanate)

There are many variations of this dish throughout Central Asia. Unlike kabobs, the Uzbek version of pilaf does not marinate the meat ahead of time. Nevertheless the cooking results in a tender and exotically flavored dish, one that was a great success in our Moscow restaurant before the October Revolution drove away our wealthy clientele and brought our "petty bourgeois" adventures in the culinary arts to a screeching halt.

Lamb

1/4 cup olive oil
2 pounds boneless shoulder of lamb, trimmed of fat and cut into
1-inch cubes
4 medium carrots, julienned
2 large onions, cut into strips
4 cups long-grain white rice
2 teaspoons salt, or to taste
1/2 teaspoon finely ground black pepper
7 cups of water or stock, lamb or vegetable
1 cup finely chopped green onions

SERVES 4 TO 6.

In a large, heavy pan, heat the oil and stir in the lamb. Turn constantly and cook for 6 minutes until lightly browned on all sides. Transfer to a separate bowl. Add the carrots and onions to the pan, stirring constantly until they are soft and supple, but not brown. Add the rice and stir. Reduce the heat and stir for 2 to 3 minutes until the grains of rice are coated with oil. Sprinkle with salt and pepper.

Stir in the meat and add the water. Raise the heat until the liquid boils. Cover tightly and simmer for 25 minutes until the cooking liquid is absorbed.

Sprinkle with green onions. Serve with *non*, flat onion bread (page 68).

Mustard Roasted Leg of Lamb
Honiny Mah
(KHANATE OF THE GREAT KHAN)

Here's a more pungent approach to cooking lamb. A favorite among Mongols living in China, ethnic Chinese generally scorn lamb or mutton for its strong flavor. Whenever one finds lamb on the menu of a Chinese restaurant, rest assured that the recipe is of Mongolian or Inner Mongolian origin. This preparation was one of my grandfather's favorites and occasionally appeared on the London menu as a special.

Lamb

1/2 cup Chinese mustard, hot or mild
2 tablespoons mushroom soy sauce
2 tablespoons crushed garlic
1 teaspoon coarsely chopped fresh thyme
3/4 tablespoon finely grated ginger
2 tablespoons vegetable oil
2 tablespoons rice wine or dry sherry
dash of chili oil, or to taste
5 to 6 pound leg of lamb
1 cup finely chopped green onions

SERVES 8 TO 10.

Preheat the oven to 350 degrees F for 10 minutes before cooking.

Place the mustard, soy sauce, garlic, thyme, ginger, vegetable oil, wine, and chili oil in a blender. Mix until smooth and creamy. Then brush over the lamb and allow to marinate for 4 hours, turning and basting every 30 minutes.

Place the lamb on a tray and roast for 2 to 2 1/2 hours, or longer, if necessary, turning frequently and basting with the juices from the bottom of the pan. Slice finely and serve with rice or plain buns.

Sprinkle with chopped green onions. Serve over a bed of rice.

Imperial Mongolian Cooking

Red Lamb

Honiny Mah Ulaan

(KHANATE OF THE GREAT KHAN)

Traditionally made with breast of lamb cut into small pieces, this recipe from Chinese Inner Mongolia can be somewhat greasy. For this reason it was carefully modified by my grandfather. Not only does leg of lamb have a lower fat content than the breast, it is more delicate and tender. The shiitake mushrooms lend the dish a dark, smoky flavor. Although fresh shiitake mushrooms can be used, the recipe works best using the dried variety.

Lamb

> **6 dried shiitake mushrooms**
> **4 pounds leg of lamb, cut into 1-inch cubes**
> **2 tablespoons vegetable oil**
> **1 large onion, cut into wedges**
> **1/2 cup mushroom soy sauce**
> **1 teaspoon salt, or to taste**
> **1 teaspoon finely grated ginger**
> **2 red bell peppers, thinly sliced**

SERVES 6 TO 8.

Soak the mushrooms in 2 cups of water until soft. Meanwhile, brown the lamb in the oil in a heavy pan and pour off any fat or oil. Strain the mushroom soaking liquid and add it to the pan. Bring to a boil. Then add the onion, soy sauce, salt, and ginger. Reduce the heat, cover, and let the lamb simmer for 3 hours, adding a little water if the stew begins to dry out.

Stem and slice the mushrooms. Add to the stew and cook for 30 minutes. Stir in the bell peppers and cook for 15 minutes.

Serve with rice and side salad.

Lhasa Lamb Curry

Lugshae Goptse

(KHANATE OF THE GREAT KHAN)

Tibetan curries differ from those of India. Favoring a subtle blend of spices, Tibetan curries are never overpowering. This recipe originated in India and was adopted by Tibetan trader, brought to Lhasa and adapted to suit local palates. A festive dish, it is served in wealthy houses on special occasions.

Lamb

1/2 teaspoon powdered cumin
1 tablespoon crushed red chili pepper, or to taste
1/2 teaspoon turmeric
1 teaspoon grated ginger
2 pounds lean lamb, cut into 1-inch cubes
1/2 cup plus 2 tablespoons vegetable oil
1/2 teaspoon whole fenugreek seeds
3/4 cup finely chopped onions
2 to 3 finely chopped shallots
1 tablespoon finely chopped garlic
4 medium carrots, sliced
1 cup coarsely chopped tomatoes
1 cup thinly sliced green bell pepper

SERVES 4.

In a large nonmetal mixing bowl, blend the cumin, chili pepper, turmeric, and ginger. Add the meat and 1/2 cup of the vegetable oil. Cover and marinate for 3 to 4 hours.

Heat the remaining 2 tablespoons of oil in a heavy saucepan and stir in the fenugreek seeds, cooking until they turn dark brown. Stir in the onions, shallots, and garlic, cooking until browned. Lower the heat to medium and stir in the lamb. Cook for 5 minutes, stirring constantly. Add the carrots, tomatoes, and 1/2 cup water. Stir well and cover. Cook for 15 minutes until the meat and vegetables are tender. Add the bell pepper, cook for 5 minutes and serve over a bed of rice.

Tibetan Meatball Curry

Shabril

(KHANATE OF THE GREAT KHAN)

Regarded as a festive dish, *shabril* is a Tibetan delicacy reserved for honored guests and special occasions. Although a wide variety of mushrooms grow in Tibet, commercially raised white mushrooms, crimini, or shiitake mushrooms are all perfectly suitable. Traditionally, the dish is thickened with milk of staggering fat content that comes from a crossbreed of yak and cow, called the *dzomo*. Sour cream or plain yogurt work perfectly well and are far more healthful.

Lamb

2 pounds ground lamb
4 teaspoons vegetable oil
1/4 teaspoon fenugreek seeds
1/2 cup finely chopped onions
1 teaspoon grated ginger
1 tablespoon crushed garlic
1/2 teaspoon turmeric
salt to taste
1 tablespoon mushroom soy sauce
2 cups finely sliced mushrooms
1 cup finely sliced radishes
1 cup sour cream or plain yogurt
1/2 cup finely chopped green onions

SERVES 6 TO 8.

Roll the ground lamb into 1/2-inch balls. Heat the oil in a heavy saucepan and stir in the fenugreek seeds, cooking until they turn dark brown. Stir in the onions and cook until golden brown. Lower the heat to medium and gently stir in the lamb. Stir in the ginger, garlic, turmeric, salt, and soy sauce. Add a little water, if necessary. Cover, reduce heat, and simmer for 5 minutes.

Stir in the mushrooms and radishes, cooking for 15 minutes or until tender. Remove the pan from the heat and gently stir in the sour cream. Sprinkle with green onions.

Serve with rice and *baistsaa*, spicy cabbage (page 169).

Tartar Lamb Dumplings

Chebureki

(CHAGHADAI KHANATE)

Lamb

Before their armies were annihilated by Genghis Khan, the Tatars were a dominant Mongolian tribe. The few survivors were incorporated into the Mongol Empire and the two became associated in Western mind. As warriors the Mongols were so ferocious, the first Europeans who had contact with them nicknamed them "Tartars," a medieval pun since the Latin word for hell is *tartarus*.

This version comes from Uzbekistan, where it remains a popular dish. The modified recipe below has been in my family for over a century.

PELMENI DOUGH:

1 3/4 cups all-purpose flour
salt to taste
1 egg

Sift the flour in a large bowl, then add the salt. Make a well in the center and break the egg, pouring it into the well. Use a fork to mix into a stiff paste, adding a little water at a time. Knead the mixture on a floured board until it is smooth. Roll it about 1/8 inch thick.

FILLING:

3 tablespoons butter or margarine
1 tablespoon vegetable oil
3/4 pound finely ground lamb
1/4 cup coarsely chopped parsley
2 tablespoons finely chopped cilantro
3 tablespoons cooked long-grain white rice, cold
2 teaspoons salt, or to taste
1 egg, lightly beaten
vegetable oil for deep-frying

SERVES 4 TO 6.

Imperial Mongolian Cooking

For the filling, melt the butter in the vegetable oil in a heavy pan set over high heat. Stir in the ground lamb and cook for 5 minutes. Transfer to a mixing bowl and blend in the parsley, cilantro, rice, and salt, blending thoroughly. Set aside and allow to cool to room temperature.

Place the dough over the back of your hands and spread until the dough stretches and is almost paper thin. Lay it on the table and use a 3-inch cookie cutter to make 74 rounds.

Add a teaspoon of the filling to half of the rounds then flatten slightly. Cover with the remaining rounds. Seal the edges by pressing with a fork. Then lightly brush the dumpling with the beaten egg.

Heat the vegetable oil for deep frying to 375 degrees F. Fry 5 dumplings at a time for 2 to 3 three minutes, turning to make sure they're evenly browned. Drain on paper towels and serve piping hot with rice and a side salad.

Lamb and Apricot Stew

Missov Dziran

(The Ilkhanate)

Armenians know the harsh winter of Central Asia means an end to fresh fruit. In summer, fruit is dried and stored in vast quantities before the onset of the cold season. The use of dried apricots, nuts, and lamb produces a dish that is truly memorable. This recipe was one of the most requested items at the family restaurant. It is one of my favorites.

Lamb

> 2 tablespoons vegetable oil
> 1 medium onion, finely chopped
> 1 tablespoon crushed garlic
> 1 pound boneless leg of lamb, cut into 1-inch cubes
> 1 tablespoon lemon juice, freshly squeezed and strained
> 2 cups lamb or vegetable stock
> 1 teaspoon grated ginger
> salt and black pepper, to taste
> 1 cup dried apricots
> 1 tablespoons coarsely chopped walnuts
> 1 to 2 tablespoons honey

Serves 4.

In a heavy saucepan, heat the oil and stir in the onion and garlic, sautéing until soft but not brown. Add the lamb and stir constantly, until browned all over. Stir in the lemon juice, stock, ginger, salt, and pepper. Reduce the heat, add the apricots, walnuts, and honey. Mix thoroughly with a wooden spoon. Cover and simmer for 20 minutes until both the meat and the fruit are tender.

Serve with rice and warm bread.

Spicy Lamb with Shredded Green Onions

Songino Honiny Mah

(KHANATE OF THE GREAT KHAN)

Originally, this dish called for mutton, a favorite of the Mongols of Inner Mongolia. Mutton is more subtle but its texture can be coarse. For this reason, it is not easily obtained in America. Besides, it is far better and richer when prepared with lean, well-trimmed lamb.

Lamb

> *1 pound boneless, lean lamb*
> *3 bunches green onions*
> *2 tablespoons sherry*
> *1 tablespoon soy sauce*
> *1 tablespoon cornstarch*
> *1/4 cup vegetable oil*
> *1 teaspoon salt, or to taste*
> *1/2 teaspoon sugar*

SERVES 4.

Slice the lamb into sections 1 1/2 inches long by 1/4 inch wide and 1/4 inch thick. Then cut green onions into 2-inch lengths. Mix the sherry, soy sauce, and cornstarch together. Marinate the lamb in the seasoning mixture for 15 minutes.

In a wok or heavy saucepan, heat half the oil and stir-fry the green onions until they wilt. Stir in the salt and sugar. Remove from the wok and set aside.

Add the remaining oil to the wok or pan. When it is sufficiently hot, stir in the lamb shreds and cook for 3 to 4 minutes. Stir in the green onions. Cook for an additional minute.

Serve with rice and thin slices of raw carrots and red peppers.

Lamb and Eggplant à la Genghis Khan

Honiny Mah Chinggis Khan

(KHANATE OF THE GREAT KHAN)

This dish is often served during the Festival of the Harvest Moon in Chinese-controlled Inner Mongolia. It is rarely enjoyed in the newly democratized Republic of Mongolia since most vegetables are grown in hothouses and are quite scarce. Tomatoes take priority over eggplants for Mongolian farmers, making this dish hard to come by in its country of origin. Although it is rare, it is a truly tempting dish blending the rich, full-bodied flavor of lamb with the subtle taste and texture of eggplant.

Lamb

4 tablespoons vegetable oil
1 teaspoon lemon juice
1 tablespoon crushed garlic
2 pounds boneless leg of lamb, cut into 1-inch cubes
2 teaspoons salt, or to taste
1 teaspoon freshly ground black pepper
1 medium onion, finely sliced
1 eggplant, peeled, quartered, and sliced
1 tablespoon soy sauce
1 cup lamb or vegetable stock
1 tablespoon cornstarch, optional

SERVE 6 TO 8.

Mix 1 tablespoon of the oil and the lemon juice. Rub the garlic into the lamb and place it in the oil mixture. Season with salt and pepper. Add the sliced onion and mix thoroughly. Cover and allow to marinate in the refrigerator overnight.

In a wok or heavy saucepan, heat the remaining 3 tablespoons of vegetable oil. Dry the lamb with paper towels. Then stir in the lamb and brown. Add the eggplant, stirring constantly for 2 minutes. Stir in the onion, garlic, and marinating liquid. Add the soy sauce and the stock. Reduce heat, cover, and simmer for 15 minutes. If the cooking liquid isn't thick enough, add the cornstarch dissolved in an equal amount of water. Stir in and cook until the liquid thickens.

Serve with rice or steamed buns (plain or lamb filled) and *sipen mardur*, Tibetan hot sauce (page 64).

Fried Sliced Lamb

Chung Pao Yang Jou P'ien
(KHANATE OF THE GREAT KHAN)

Lamb

This dish was introduced into the Hopei province by nomads south of the Great Wall that separates China from Mongolia. Richly flavored and aromatic, it is quick and easy to prepare. The dish comes from Inner Mongolia and shows a cross-pollination between cultures. Traditional Mongols do not stir-fry their food and the use of cooking wine comes from years of Chinese influence. On the other hand, this dish is sometimes found on Chinese menus, but most ethnic Chinese dislike lamb for its strong favor and odor. However, the British love lamb and this recipe found favor in my grandfather's London restaurant as an off-menu special.

> *1 tablespoon cornstarch*
> *1 pound leg of lamb, sliced paper thin*
> *12 green onions*
> *1 red bell pepper*
> *1/2 cup vegetable oil*
> *1 tablespoon crushed garlic*
> *1 tablespoon soy sauce*
> *1/2 teaspoon salt, or to taste*
> *1 1/2 tablespoons rice wine or sherry*
> *2 teaspoons sesame oil*

SERVES 4 TO 6.

In a mixing bowl, blend the cornstarch and 1 tablespoon water. Add the lamb and cover. Cut the green onions diagonally into 1-inch sections. Slice a red bell pepper into strips 2 inches long and 1/4 inch wide.

Heat 1/4 cup of the oil in a large saucepan or wok until moderately hot. Stir-fry the lamb for 2 minutes. Remove from the heat and place on a plate. Add the remaining 1/4 cup oil and stir in the green onions, bell peppers, and garlic. Cook for 2 minutes. Return the lamb to the saucepan and stir. Add the soy sauce, salt, and wine. Raise the heat to high and stir-fry for 1 minute. Stir in the sesame oil and cook for 1 minute or less.

Imperial Mongolian Cooking

Double-fried Lamb with Honey
T'a Ssu Mi
(KHANATE OF THE GREAT KHAN)

It is believed that this dish was developed in the kitchens of Khubilai Khan, the last of the Great Khans and by far the most enlightened. It is often bar-becued, but this version calls for it to be stir-fried, which is probably a Chinese contribution to the Imperial court. Centuries later, it remains a pop-ular dish in Chinese-controlled Inner Mongolia and in some of Beijing's more fashionable restaurants. The recipe came from Grandfather's Mongolia days. An avid collector of exotic recipes, this dish never appeared on his menu although he enjoyed preparing it for his family.

Lamb

3 1/2 tablespoons cornstarch
1 tablespoon soy jam
1 teaspoon sugar
1 pound lean leg of lamb, thinly sliced
3 tablespoons water or lamb stock
1 teaspoon finely grated ginger
2 tablespoons mushroom soy sauce
1 tablespoon rice wine vinegar
2 tablespoons sherry
4 teaspoons honey
3/4 cup vegetable oil
1 tablespoon sesame oil
1 tablespoon sesame seeds

SERVES 4 TO 6.

In a large mixing bowl, blend 5 1/4 teaspoons cornstarch with the soy jam and sugar. Stir in the lamb until it is coated.

In a separate bowl, add the remaining 5 1/4 teaspoons cornstarch to the water. Add the ginger, soy sauce, vinegar, sherry, and honey. Stir and mix thoroughly.

-CONTINUED-

In a large saucepan, heat the vegetable oil. Stir in the lamb and fry for 20 seconds, stirring constantly. Then remove from the lamb from the heat and set aside. Drain the lamb of excess oil. Discard the oil in the pan and return it to the heat. Add the drained lamb to the pan, then stir in the soy sauce mixture. Stir-fry over high heat for 10 seconds. Pour in the sesame oil and stir. Cook for 5 seconds. Remove from the heat, cover tightly and allow to sit for 5 minutes before serving. Garnish with sesame seeds.

Grilled Marinated Lamb, Georgian-style

Basturma

(KHANATE OF THE GOLDEN HORDE)

Generally, this traditional Georgian dish is marinated overnight to give the meat a deep, rich flavor. Although this recipe calls for lamb, beef, pork, or venison can be substituted. The dish is best grilled over a bed of hot coals. It is similar to *shashlyk* (page 98) and was equally popular in both of our family restaurants.

Lamb

> *2 cups pomegranate juice*
> *1/4 cup vegetable oil*
> *1 teaspoon salt, plus additional for eggplant*
> *black pepper to taste*
> *1 bay leaf, crushed*
> *1 tablespoon minced or crushed garlic*
> *2 pounds leg of lamb, cut into 2-inch cubes*
> *1 large eggplant*

SERVES 6 TO 8.

Mix the pomegranate juice with the oil, 1 teaspoon of the salt, the pepper, bay leaf, and garlic. Marinate the lamb cubes for 8 hours. Turn frequently to make sure all sides of the meat absorb the marinade equally.

Cut the eggplant into 2-inch cubes. Place on paper towels and sprinkle generously with salt. Meanwhile, heat the coals until they become white around the edges. Using clean paper towels, remove the brownish bitter juices that form on the eggplant after 30 minutes to 1 hour.

Place alternating pieces of lamb and eggplant on skewers and grill over hot coals for 10 to 15 minutes.

Serve with rice and *tkemeli* Georgian sauce (page 58).

Lamb Pilaf
Uzbek Plov
(CHAGHADAI KHANATE)

Today Uzbekistan is best known for its fabulous carpets, fertile valleys, and oil-rich fields. It once was the empire of a rich and powerful Central Asian overlord who foolishly ran afoul of Genghis Khan and paid the price. Driven from his land and divested of his wealth, he died a broken man with only rags upon his back.

Lamb

His empire was given to the youngest son of Genghis Khan, Chaghadai, a controversial move as Chaghadai's parentage was suspect. Centuries later, Uzbekistan gave rise to another fearsome warlord, Tamerlane, in whose veins Mongolian blood flowed.

While *Uzbek plov* is enjoyed throughout the Russias, especially the southern states, this delightful and delicate recipe was introduced to the family restaurant in Moscow by my ubiquitous Great Uncle Ilya.

1/4 cup olive oil
2 onions, finely chopped
1 1/2 pounds leg of lamb, trimmed of fat and cubed
3/4 pound carrots, finely chopped
1/4 teaspoon ground cinnamon
4 strands saffron, soaked in 1 teaspoon water
pinch of finely ground cardamom
2 cups long-grain white rice
salt and black pepper, to taste
3/4 cup finely chopped parsley

SERVES 10 TO 12.

Heat the oil in a large, heavy pan and add the chopped onion, stirring until lightly browned. Stir in the lamb and brown on all sides. Next, stir in the carrots, cinnamon, saffron, and cardamom. Lower the heat, cover, and simmer for 45 minutes, stirring frequently. Add a little water, if necessary.

Imperial Mongolian Cooking

Remove the cover and stir in the rice along with 4 cups of water. Add salt and pepper. Cover tightly and simmer for 15 to 20 minutes until the rice is plump and tender and no water remains.

Serve in small warmed bowls and garnish with chopped parsley.

Beef

Tibetan Steamed Rice With Beef

Trinru

(KHANATE OF THE GREAT KHAN)

Although *trinru* is often made with pork, the main source of meat in Tibet is the yak. Yak meat resembles beef, which makes a perfectly good substitute. *Trinru*, which is never eaten by nomads or farmers, is regarded as a dish for Lhasa's wealthy elite.

Beef

1 1/2 cups long-grain white rice
1/2 cup finely chopped celery
1/2 cup finely chopped onion
1/2 cup finely sliced radishes
2 tablespoons soy sauce
salt to taste
1 pound beef, cut into thin strips

SERVES 4 TO 6.

Wash and boil the rice in 3 cups of water for 15 minutes. Add the celery, onion, radishes, soy sauce, and salt. Blend the ingredients together. Place the meat into a large ceramic bowl or upper section of a double boiler. Add the rice and vegetables. Place inside a steamer or double boiler. Cover tightly. Cook for 10 to 12 minutes. Remove from the heat and transfer to a large serving dish.

Spicy Grilled Beef
Sha Katsa Chesha
(KHANATE OF THE GREAT KHAN)

This dish is enjoyed by urbanites and nomads alike. It is simple to prepare, although the necessary ingredients are not always available in Tibet, where spices have traditionally been imported from India and Bhutan. Unlike Mongolians, the Tibetan diet is centered around beeflike yak, not lamb or mutton. The version my grandfather learned was for mutton, a Mongolian adaptation he modified for European palates. He hoped to bring the recipe back home, but soon found himself smuggled out of Russia to settle in England.

Beef

1/2 cup coarsely chopped tomatoes
1 tablespoon crushed red chili pepper, or to taste
1 tablespoon crushed garlic
1 shallot, finely chopped
1/2 teaspoon turmeric
1 teaspoon grated ginger
salt to taste
2 tablespoons vegetable oil
1/4 cup finely chopped cilantro
2 pounds lean beef
1/2 cup finely chopped green onions

SERVES 6 TO 8.

Place the tomatoes, chili pepper, garlic, shallot, turmeric, ginger, and salt in a blender. Blend on high speed until smooth. Heat the oil in a pan. Stir-fry the cilantro for 2 minutes. Gently stir in the mixture from the blender and cook for an additional 2 minutes. Reduce temperature to low, cover and keep warm.

Cut the meat into 1-inch strips. Cook the meat over hot coals. When the meat is done, cover it with the sauce and garnish with green onions.

Spicy Himalayan Meat Pastry
Shapale
(KHANATE OF THE GREAT KHAN)

Although this recipe calls for meat, it is often made wild mushrooms, mustard greens, and other vegetables, which are usually fried in a little oil before being put into the pastry. Hot *shapale* make an ideal first course or it can be served with rice and vegetables as a main meal. My grandfather used to call this dish "Mongol *piroshoki*," a term he used affectionately.

Beef

FILLING:

>   2 pounds ground beef
>   2 cups finely chopped green onion
>   1/2 cup finely chopped red onion
>   salt to taste
>   1 teaspoon finely ground cumin
>   1/2 teaspoon powdered nutmeg
>   1 teaspoon freshly grated ginger
>   1/2 cup hot water

DOUGH:

>   3 cups whole-wheat flour
>   3 cups all-purpose flour
>   1 teaspoon baking powder

SERVES 6 *TO* 8.

Preheat the oven to 325 degrees F for 10 minutes.

Place the beef in a large plastic mixing bowl. Add the green onions, red onions, salt, cumin, nutmeg, and ginger. Add the water and mix thoroughly.

In a separate bowl, combine the flours and baking powder. Add a little cold water and knead until the dough become stiff. Break off a 1/2 cup of dough and roll it on a lightly floured board until it is flat and round.

Imperial Mongolian Cooking

Put half a cup of the meat mixture in the center and flatten it. Place another dough circle on top. Pinch the edges. When all the dough and meat mixture have been formed into pastries, brush the top of each with a little water.

Bake for 50 minutes or until the pastries are golden brown. Serve piping hot with a side salad such as *yaba* (page 51).

Sino-Mongolian Simmered Beef

Wei Niu Jou

(KHANATE OF THE GREAT KHAN)

Introduced by the Mongol khans, this dish is popular not only in Inner Mongolia but throughout northwest China. The use of dried tangerine peel with beef reflects Chinese influence but lends a delightful, delicate touch to this exotic dish. My grandfather's Russian patrons liked to order the dish as change of pace, washed down with prodigious amounts of vodka.

Beef

> *3 pounds boneless beef shanks*
> *1/4 cup vegetable oil*
> *2 teaspoons sugar*
> *1/4 cup sherry or rice wine*
> *2 teaspoons dried tangerine peel, soaked and drained*
> *1/4 cup finely chopped onions*
> *2 tablespoons soy sauce*
> *1 teaspoon grated ginger*
> *salt to taste*

SERVES 6 TO 8.

Cut the beef into 1-inch cubes. In a heavy saucepan, heat the oil and stir-fry the beef for 4 minutes over medium heat. Place the meat in a pan of boiling water and cook for 3 minutes. Remove the meat and drain.

Put the beef in a heavy saucepan and cover with cold water. Add the sugar, sherry, tangerine peel, onion, soy sauce, and ginger. Bring to a boil and reduce to a gentle simmer. Cover and cook at low heat for 4 hours, stirring every 30 minutes. Add salt to taste.

Serve with rice or noodles and a side salad.

Barbecued Steak, Tartar-style

Tatar Uhriin Mah

(Khanate of the Great Khan)

The very words "steak tartare" conjure images of raw meat. During their encounters with the Mongols, European observers noted that the khan's warriors would place slabs of boneless meat under their horses' saddles. Medieval Europeans assumed the purpose was to tenderize the meat which was later eaten raw. In reality, the meat under the saddles was used the help heal wounds caused by the saddle chaffing against the animal's hide. This version, a success in my grandfather's London and Moscow restaurants, is quick and simple to make.

Beef

2 pounds lean, boneless beef steak
1/2 cup finely chopped green onions
1 tablespoon finely chopped garlic
2 tablespoons soy sauce
2 teaspoons soy jam
1/4 teaspoon dry mustard
1 teaspoon sesame oil

Serves 6 to 8.

Braise the steaks over hot coals until done to taste. Meanwhile, blend the green onions, garlic, soy sauce, soy jam, mustard, and sesame oil. Smother the steak in the sauce mixture and serve with rice and any vegetable side dish.

Mongolian Fried Steak

Ho Chien Pao Jou

(KHANATE OF THE GREAT KHAN)

To ensure success one must use a high-quality, tender cut of beef cut into thin slices across the grain. The recipe, like most Mongol beef dishes, hails from Inner Mongolia. Adopted by the Chinese population, even the dish's name is Chinese. As the quality of beef in Russia, past and present, is poor, my grandfather seldom featured the dish. When my grandfather discovered Scottish beef, he was overjoyed and gladly offered this tasty dish to his patrons.

Beef

> *2 pounds 1-inch thick boneless steak, trimmed of fat*
> *3 tablespoons mushroom soy sauce*
> *1 tablespoon cornstarch*
> *2 cups vegetable oil*
> *1 tablespoon crushed garlic*
> *1 cup finely chopped green onions*
> *1 tablespoon sherry or rice wine*
> *2 teaspoons rice wine vinegar*

SERVES 8.

Place the beef in a bowl with 1 1/2 tablespoons of the soy sauce and the cornstarch. Mix thoroughly. Heat the oil in a heavy saucepan or a wok. Stir in the beef and cook for 1 minute. Remove the beef from the wok and set aside. Stir in the garlic and green onions, frying over high heat until browned. Return the beef to the wok and stir in the sherry, 1 tablespoon water, the vinegar and remaining 1 1/2 tablespoons soy sauce. Cook for 1 minute.

Serve with rice and *baitsaa*, a spicy Mongolian preparation of red cabbage and mushrooms (page 169).

Armenian Fried Meat Patties

Dabgvadz Keufteh

(THE ILKHANATE)

These delicately spiced beef patties are an unusual culinary treats for Armenian meat recipes generally call for lamb. The meat must be finely ground, usually twice. The texture should be more like a thick paste rather than American-style ground beef. The dish is more Middle Eastern than Byzantine, but the results are delightful and brought my grandfather many compliments.

Beef

2 pounds lean ground beef
1 large onion, grated
4 slices white bread, trimmed of crusts and soaked in water for
30 minutes and squeezed
2 eggs
1/2 cup finely chopped parsley
1 teaspoon ground cinnamon
1 tablespoon finely chopped garlic
salt to taste
1/2 teaspoon freshly ground black pepper
1/2 cup all-purpose flour
3 tablespoons vegetable oil

SERVES 8.

In a large plastic mixing bowl, combine the beef, onion, bread, eggs, parsley, cinnamon, garlic, salt, and pepper. Mix thoroughly. Moisten your hands and shape the meat into flat round patties 2 inches in diameter. Roll gently in flour.

In a heavy saucepan, heat the oil. Fry at moderate temperature, turning until golden brown on both sides.

Serve with lightly buttered egg noodles and a side salad.

Melon Stuffed With Spicy Beef
Missov Sekhi Dolma
(CHAGHADAI KHANATE)

Beef

Throughout Central Asia and Asia Minor, a variety of fruits and vegetables are served stuffed ranging from vine leaves in Greece to zucchini in Turkey and melons in Uzbekistan and Armenia. This version uses cantaloupe and a stuffing of beef, dried fruits, nuts, and spices. Brought back by Great Uncle Ilya, an Uzbek official who swore that while the Armenians claimed to have created the dish, it was originally developed in Samarkand in the thirteenth century. While difficult to prove, this may be true as medieval Uzbekistan was famous for its melons, which were packed in ice and exported in lead boxes.

> *1 large cantaloupe, not overripe*
> *2 tablespoons butter*
> *1/2 pound lean ground beef*
> *1 medium onion, finely chopped*
> *1/2 cup long-grain white rice*
> *1/4 cup coarsely chopped walnuts*
> *1/4 cup dried currants*
> *1/2 teaspoon finely ground cinnamon*
> *salt and pepper, to taste*
> *1 cup beef broth*

SERVES 4.

Preheat the oven to 350 degrees F for 10 minutes before cooking.

Lightly brush a baking pan with vegetable oil. Slice off the top of the cantaloupe (about 1 inch should do), set aside for later use. Remove the seeds and pulp from the interior of the melon. Scoop out 1 cup of the melon flesh and chop coarsely.

Imperial Mongolian Cooking

Melt the butter in a heavy saucepan. Stir in the beef and onion, sautéing over medium heat until browned. Add the rice, walnuts, currants, cinnamon, salt, pepper, and beef broth. Cover and cook until the liquid in the pan is absorbed and the rice is tender, about 20 minutes. Remove from the heat. Allow to cool.

When the meat mixture cools to room temperature, stuff the melon and cover with the top, holding it in place with wooden toothpicks.

Place the cantaloupe in the center of the pan and bake for an hour or until completely tender. Serve with plenty of warm flat bread such as *non* (page 68).

Meat Dumplings à la Tamerlane
Manty
(CHAGADAI KHANATE)

While most often made with lamb, *manty* is equally delicious when made with beef. Eaten in Armenia, Uzbekistan, and other parts of Central Asia, it is believed that *manty* was introduced by the warriors of the Mongolian steppes. The Armenians also make an interesting version. Small *manty* can be served as an appetizer, which was my grandfather's approach, but I prefer it as a main dish.

Beef

FILLING:
> 1 1/2 pounds lean ground beef
> 1 1/2 cups finely chopped onions
> 2 teaspoons salt, or to taste
> 1/2 teaspoon freshly ground black pepper
> 7 tablespoons vegetable oil

DOUGH:
> 3 cups all-purpose flour
> 1/4 cup finely chopped fresh dill leaves
> 3/4 cup plain yogurt

SERVES 4 TO 6.

Mix the beef, onions, salt, and pepper. Blend well to combine.

In a separate mixing bowl, pour in the flour and make a well in the center. Pour 1 1/2 cups of water into the well. Mix until smooth, then form the dough into a ball and place on a lightly floured wooden board. Roll into a rectangle approximately 1/16 inch thick. Use a 5-inch cookie cutter and cut 15 to 20 circles of dough. Place 5 teaspoons of filling on each. Moisten the top with a little vegetable oil. Raise the sides of the circle until they meet in the middle. Moisten your fingers with water and pinch the top closed, then twist it to form a pouch.

In the bottom of a steamer, bring an inch of water to a boil. Place the *manty* in the perforated steamer insert, cover tightly and reduce the heat. Steam for 15 minutes and sprinkle with dill.

Serve with yogurt over a bed of rice.

Barbecued Beefsteak, Tartar-style

Hou Jou

(KHANATE OF THE GREAT KHAN)

Beef

Often served in Beijing, this recipe originates from the Mongol hordes that controlled China until 1368. The Chinese version calls for ham steak. Beef makes an excellent substitute. This version was part of my grandfather's repertoire. To the best of my knowledge it never appeared on the menus of his restaurants in Moscow and London, but it was served at family get-togethers.

> *1 teaspoon finely grated scallions*
> *1 teaspoon crushed garlic*
> *2 tablespoons mushroom soy sauce*
> *2 tablespoons soy jam*
> *1/4 teaspoon dry mustard*
> *1/2 teaspoon chili oil, or to taste*
> *1 teaspoon sesame oil*
> *2 pounds boneless beefsteak*

SERVES 6 TO 8.

Combine the scallions, garlic, soy sauce, soy jam, dry mustard, and chili and sesame oils. Mix thoroughly.

Cook the steaks over an open fire or hot coals until the meat is done to taste.

Brush with the sauce and serve with rice and sliced raw vegetables of your choosing.

Mongolian Meat Pancakes

Huushuur

(KHANATE OF THE GREAT KHAN)

Curiously, a favorite with the lunch crowd in London, this dish is usually made with lamb or mutton, but I have modified the recipe for beef. A vegetarian form of the dish is eaten in Tibet. This traditional Mongolian meat-filled pancake is a hearty and sustaining meal in itself. It is believed to date back to the era of Genghis Khan and today is often served in the felt-covered *gers* that dot the Mongolian landscape.

Beef

FILLING:

1/2 pound lean ground beef
4 tablespoons vegetable oil
1/2 cup finely chopped onions
2 teaspoons crushed garlic
1 teaspoon grated ginger
1/4 teaspoon powdered turmeric
1/3 teaspoon powdered cumin
10 drops red chili oil, or to taste
salt to taste

BATTER:

1 cup all-purpose flour
1 egg
1 egg yolk
1 cup milk
1 tablespoon butter, melted
6 tablespoons vegetable oil for griddle

SERVES 4.

Place the beef in a large, nonmetallic mixing bowl and add 2 tablespoons of oil, the onions, garlic, ginger, turmeric, cumin, chili oil, and salt. Form into patties.

-CONTINUED-

In a heavy saucepan, heat the remaining 2 tablespoons of oil and brown the beef. Remove from the heat and place on a warm plate. Meanwhile, sift the flour with a pinch of salt. Make a well in the center and drop in the egg and egg yolk. Add 1/2 cup of the milk to the egg and gently stir into the flour. Beat and stir the butter. Whisk in the remaining 1/2 cup of the milk, cover and keep in a cool, draft-free place for 30 minutes.

On a lightly oiled griddle or in a large heavy saucepan, pour 1/2 teaspoon of batter into the center of the pan and spread it around. Then pour 1/2 cup of the batter into the middle. Again, spread it around until it is flat. Repeat the process so that you have two pancakes cooking at the same time. Add a beef patty to one of the pancakes while it is still undercooked and the open side is slightly runny. Flip the second pancake on top of the one containing the meat.

Turn over and heat until it is cooked through. Serve piping hot.

Mongolian
Hot Pot &
Cooking Stocks

Introduction to Hot Pot Cookery

Used widely throughout Inner Mongolia and Northern China, it is known as the Firepot, Chrysanthemum Pot (when chrysanthemum petals are used in the process of cooking), and the Mongolian Hot Pot. The Mongolian Hot Pot, a brass chafing pot for simmering the stock in which food is cooked, is perfect for winter cooking and parties. The pot is fueled by charcoal or alcohol with a funnel running down the center, which heats the large bowl surrounding it to produce high temperatures for fast cooking.

The hot pot must be placed on a heavy wooden board to prevent its heat from damaging the table. Stock is poured into the bowl along with a variety of vegetables and noodles.

Plates of raw vegetables and thinly sliced meat, fish, or chicken are placed on the dinning table along with a variety of dishes filled with dipping sauces. The diners are given a set of chopsticks or a wire mesh strainer and individual plates, including separate soup bowls and soup spoons. Each diner picks up a slice of meat and plunges it into the pot to cook for a minute or two. The meat is then dipped into one or more of the sauces and eaten.

Everything begins with the broth. Mongolians use a hearty lamb stock complemented by dumplings, buns, or steamed breads. A common Chinese practice is to add a half pound of parboiled peastarch noodles to the broth halfway through the meal. When all the meat and vegetables have been eaten, the diners help themselves to the stock and noodles, finishing the meal with a rich noodle soup.

Chicken Stock

Gai Tong

(KHANATE OF THE GREAT KHAN)

This stock is simple to make and can be used in Chinese chicken and fish dishes, as well Mongolian hot pot cookery.

Mongolian
Hot Pot &
Cooking
Stocks

1 chicken (3 to 4 pounds), skinned
3 slices gingerroot
1 leek
2 cups chopped carrots
2 cups chopped cabbage
2 cups chopped turnips
2 cups chopped celery
2 cups finely sliced mushrooms
2 cups finely sliced onions
1 teaspoon salt
1 teaspoon mushroom soy sauce
1 tablespoon sherry

MAKES ENOUGH STOCK FOR 1 CROCKPOT MEAL.

Place the chicken in a large pot with 12 cups cold water and bring to a boil. Reduce the heat and skim the surface. Add the ginger slices and the leek. Cover and simmer for 2 hours. Remove the chicken from the broth.

Add the carrots, cabbage, turnips, celery, mushrooms, and onions. Simmer for 20 minutes. Finally, add the salt, soy sauce, and the sherry. Cook for 5 minutes, then strain.

Set the chicken aside as it can be used in other dishes.

To completely remove the fat, place the stock in the refrigerator overnight. A layer of fat will form on the top and can be easily removed with a ladle.

Lamb Stock

Yeung Yuk Tong

(KHANATE OF THE GREAT KHAN)

Although many Mongols living in China's Inner Mongolia Autonomous Region use water for their hot pot meals, lamb stock produces a far richer dish.

Mongolian
Hot Pot &
Cooking
Stocks

2 pounds neck of lamb

1 teaspoon salt

1 leek

2 celery stalks

2 medium white onions

1/2 cup rehydrated dried black mushrooms, stalks removed

1/2 cup sliced water chestnuts

1 teaspoon mushroom soy sauce

MAKES ENOUGH STOCK FOR 1 CROCKPOT MEAL.

Place the lamb in a pot with 12 cups water and bring to a boil. Add the salt, leek, celery, and onions. Reduce the heat and skim the surface. Cover and simmer for 90 minutes.

Slice the mushrooms and add them to the stock with the water chestnuts and soy sauce. Simmer for 30 minutes. Remove the meat and strain the broth.

Since lamb contains a fair share of fat, place the stock in the refrigerator overnight. Use a ladle to remove the layer of fat that forms on the surface.

Jnner Mongolian Lamb Hot Pot

Suan Yong Jou

(KHANATE OF THE GREAT KHAN)

The use of lamb hot pot in Northern China dates from the previous century and was introduced into Beijing by Mongolians. The lamb must be sliced paper thin and the best way to do this is to defrost a leg of lamb, cutting the meat while is it not fully thawed. This recipe is perfect for a dinner party.

Mongolian
Hot Pot &
Cooking
Stocks

HOT POT:
> *12 cups lamb stock*
> *1/2 pound peastarch noodles*
> *1 pound bok choy, sliced*
> *10 green onions, finely chopped*
> *1 pound spinach, washed and stems removed*
> *5 pounds lean lamb, sliced paper thin*

DIPS:
> *mushroom soy sauce*
> *sesame oil*
> *sipen mardur Tibetan hot sauce (page 64)*
> *Chinese mustard*
> *2 cloves garlic, ground and mixed with 1 teaspoon sugar*

BREADS:
> *bao chicken-filled buns (page 90)*
> *Kapse Tibetan fried bread (page 70)*
> *Trimomo steamed bread, Tibetan-style (page 71).*

SERVES 15 TO 20.

Place the hot pot in the center of the table. Pour in the lamb stock and bring to a boil. Meanwhile, parboil the noodles for 20 minutes. When the stock starts to boil, add 1/4 of the vegetables. Within a few minutes, the stock will return to a full boil. At this point, each guest picks up a piece of meat and immerses it in the stock. After the meat changes color, the diner plunges the meat in one or more of the dips.

-CONTINUED-

As the meal progresses, the remaining vegetables are added to the stock. At the halfway point, drop in the noodles. When all the meat is eaten, the guests can help themselves to the broth, now rich with vegetable and noodles.

Have plenty of Tibetan breads on hand.

Fish Hot Pot

Chu Hua Yu Keng Kuo

(KHANATE OF THE GREAT KHAN)

This dish originates in the Szechwan province of China, known for its hot, spicy food. This is one of the few examples of hot pot cooking that uses fish and white chrysanthemum petals, although peach and apple blossoms are often substituted. Virtually any white, non-oily fish can be used. Sole, cod, or catfish make a delicious and exotic meal.

Mongolian
Hot Pot &
Cooking
Stocks

1 1/2 cups peastarch noodles
vegetable oil for deep-frying
1/2 cup blanched almonds
4 pounds fish fillets
12 cups chicken stock
2 green onions, finely chopped
4 slices fresh gingerroot
1 teaspoon salt
1 teaspoon soy sauce
1/2 cup chrysanthemum petals, or apple or peach fruit blossoms
1 1/2 pounds chicken breasts, skinned and diced
1/2 pound boy choy, sliced
1/2 pound spinach, washed and stemmed
1 cup bean sprouts

SAUCES:
soy sauce
sesame oil
chili oil
Chinese mustard
garlic, finely crushed mixed with sugar
shrimp sauce

SERVES 15 TO 20.

Deep-fry the noodles in oil until they begin to puff up, then drain them on paper towels. In the same oil, deep-fry the almonds until they turn golden brown. Remove from the oil and drain on fresh paper towels.

Cut the fish into thin slices. Bring the chicken stock to a boil and add the green onions, ginger, salt, and soy sauce.

When the stock returns to a boil, add the chrysanthemum petals. Add the chicken. When the hot pot returns to the boil, add the almonds, bok choy, spinach, and bean sprouts. Allow the mixture to boil for 1 minute.

Slices of fish can now be cooked in the broth for a minute or two, then dipped in one of the sauces.

Serve with rice. When the fish is finished, serve the broth in soup bowls.

Mongolian Barbecue

Introduction to Mongolian Barbecue

During the early 1980s, Americans were introduced to Mongolian cuisine when a sizable number of Chinese restaurants featured the Mongolian Barbecue. Like the hot pot, the guest becomes the chef.

The technique is popular in Northern China. Cooking is done on a massive stove with an iron covering over a stack of glowing coals. Americans can get excellent results using a standard barbecue or large hibachi covered with a thin sheet of iron or a fine wire mesh.

Lamb is the basis for Mongolian barbecuing, but other meat such beef, chicken, pork, and fish, even vegetables, can be used instead. Almost any food lends itself to hot pot cooking. If you are using meat, it should be sliced paper thin. This is easier if the meat is frozen ahead of time and is sliced while still not fully defrosted.

Each guest is given a bowl or two of sauces in which the meat is marinated for a few minutes. The meat is placed on the grill and flipped back and forth using chopsticks or a spatula.

The meat is usually served with steamed buns, but rice makes a good all-around accompaniment.

Mongolian Barbecue Sauce I

Su Jeung

(KHANATE OF THE GREAT KHAN)

The Mongolian barbecue is rarely found in the Mongolian Republic itself. But it is popular in the more temperate regions of Inner Mongolia, where there are more opportunities to cook outdoors. The Mongolian barbecue is more of a covered grill than the American version. Cooking in the Mongolian Republic with its chilling Gobi winds and erratic dust storms makes an open grill impractical.

Mongolian Barbecue

When cooking outdoors, there are a few simple rules to keep in mind. Each guest is given his own bowl of sauce in which the meat is dipped and marinated before cooking. Often a series of marinades and dipping sauces are offered to each guest, who uses chopsticks to cook the dipped or marinated meat or fish. Either way it is delicious and perfect for dinner parties and get-togethers.

On warm summer days in Hulan Beir, Dorje would prepare the Mongolian barbecue with the following sauces while my grandfather and his fellow officers provided an endless stream of vodka.

Small wonder Russia lost that war.

> *1/2 cup slivered green onions*
> *1 clove garlic, crushed*
> *1/4 cup finely chopped parsley*
> *1 cup water or rice wine*
> *1/2 cup soy sauce*
> *1 tablespoon sugar*

MAKES ENOUGH SAUCE FOR 15 TO 20 DINERS.

Mix the ingredients together and allow to stand at least 15 minutes before cooking. Divide into separate bowls for each diner.

Mongolian Barbecue Sauce II

Su Jeung

(INNER MONGOLIA)

Most Mongolian meals are based around mutton or lamb. For those not fond of either, this sauce lends a delicate flavor to beef or even pork. Unlike the preceding recipe, this sauce is used to dip the meat in *after* it has been cooked.

Mongolian
Barbecue

> *4 cloves garlic, crushed*
> *4 green onions, finely chopped*
> *4 tablespoons soy sauce*
> *4 tablespoons sweet soy jam*
> *2 teaspoons chili oil, or to taste*
> *2 teaspoons sesame oil*

MAKES ENOUGH DIPPING SAUCE FOR 15 TO 20 DINERS.

Mix all ingredients together. Divide evenly among guests, each receiving one bowl. Serve with rice and finely sliced raw vegetables, such as red peppers or carrots, to garnish.

Fish & Seafood

Creamy Fish and Shellfish Sausages

Sosiski Ribny i Slifki

(KHANATE OF THE GOLDEN HORDE)

Fish & Seafood

A delicate and unusual dish, this exotic sausage is usually made in late summer when Ukrainian creeks fill with crayfish. This version makes use of more easily obtained shellfish. Like the original version, it can be prepared in advance and frozen. As a rule, my grandfather used prawns in his London restaurant as crayfish were impossible to obtain in wartorn Britain.

SAUSAGE:

1 large onion, finely chopped
3 tablespoons butter
2 pounds filleted white fish
2 pounds shelled and deveined prawns or shelled lobster tails
2 teaspoons paprika
2 teaspoons finely chopped fresh dill
1 tablespoon freshly chopped cilantro
salt to taste
1 cup heavy cream
sausage casing
1 to 2 cups milk

SAUCE:

2 tablespoons butter or margarine
2 tablespoons all-purpose flour
1 cup heavy cream
1/4 cup fish stock or clam juice
2 teaspoons tomato paste
white pepper to taste

SERVES 8 TO 10.

Sauté the onions in the butter until transparent. While the onions cool, cut the fish into 1-inch cubes. Dice the lobster or prawns. In a food processor, combine the fish, onions, paprika, dill, cilantro, and salt. Puree for 1 minute then add 1/3 cup of the cream. Puree for 2 minutes and add another 1/3 cup of cream. Add the shellfish and puree for 1 minute. Whip the remaining cream and fold into the fish mixture. Stuff the casing with the fish/cream mixture, tying the ends with string at the top and bottom. In a heavy saucepan, heat the milk and simmer the sausage for 20 minutes. Remove from the heat and cover.

To make the sauce, melt the butter and stir in the flour. Add the cream followed by the fish stock, stirring constantly. Stir in the tomato paste and white pepper.

Serve with rice and steamed carrots or red cabbage. Slice the sausages and cover with sauce. Sprinkle with a little extra paprika and white pepper.

Turkish Swordfish Kabobs
Kilic Sis
(The Ilkhanate)

Fish &
Seafood

Although variations of this dish appear in Armenia and elsewhere in the former Soviet Union, it is really a Turkish specialty. Above all, it is simple to make and delicate in flavor, especially if cooked over hot coals. As swordfish was almost impossible to obtain on a regular basis in Tsarist Russia, my family would prepare the meal with salmon or sturgeon. It is generally more successful when swordfish is used, especially if the fish is fresh.

> *2 pounds swordfish*
>
> **MARINADE:**
> *1/4 cup lemon juice, freshly squeezed and strained (1 to 2 lemons)*
> *2 tablespoons olive oil*
> *1 medium onion, sliced*
> *2 teaspoons paprika*
> *1 teaspoon salt, or to taste*
> *freshly ground black pepper to taste*
> *2 bay leaves, crumbled*
>
> **SAUCE:**
> *1/4 cup olive oil*
> *1/4 cup lemon juice, freshly squeezed and strained*
> *1/4 cup finely chopped parsley*
> *salt to taste*
> *freshly ground black pepper to taste*
>
> **SERVES 4 TO 6.**

Remove the skin from the swordfish and cut into 1/4-inch cubes.

Combine the marinade ingredients in a nonmetallic bowl. Stir in the swordfish cubes, making sure the sides of every piece are coated. Cover and refrigerate for 4 hours, turning once every 30 minutes.

Place the fish cubes on skewers and cook over glowing coals for up to 12 minutes, turning frequently and basting with the marinade.

Combine the sauce ingredients in a sealed container and shake vigorously. Serve the fish over rice and pour the sauce over the top.

Sprinkle with a little lemon juice and paprika. Serve on a warmed plate with rice, a vegetable side dish, or sliced cucumbers.

Georgian Marinated Fish

Tatris Basturma

(KHANATE OF THE GOLDEN HORDE)

It is most common to see this dish made with fresh salmon steaks, but any other firm-fleshed fish will work. Swordfish or even halibut or sturgeon are excellent prepared this way. While not a complicated dish, it is enjoyed throughout the Russias and is best grilled outdoors over glowing coals.

Fish &
Seafood

1 large onion, peeled and grated
1 teaspoon salt
freshly ground black pepper to taste
2 medium bay leaves, crushed
1 large lemon, sliced
1/4 cup vegetable oil
2 pounds fish, skinned and cut into 2-inch cubes
2 teaspoons paprika
2 green onions, finely chopped
lemon wedges to garnish

SERVES 6 TO 8.

Mix the onion, salt, pepper, bay leaves, lemon slices, and vegetable oil in a large bowl. Blend thoroughly then stir in the fish, making sure that each piece is coated on all sides. Cover and refrigerate for 5 to 6 hours.

Thread the fish onto skewers and cook over glowing coals for 10 to 12 minutes. Sprinkle the fish with paprika and green onions. Garnish with lemon wedges.

Serve with rice and a side salad.

Grilled Trout

Khorovadz Ishkhanatsoug

(The Ilkhanate)

The key to this dish is the quality and freshness of the trout used. In Armenia, the most highly prized trout are those taken from Lake Sevan, but fresh American rainbow trout are wonderfully suited to this recipe. An exotic touch is the use of pomegranate with fish. When combined with sugar, the sauce gives the dish an exotic sweet-and-sour taste and takes away some of the pomegranate's tartness.

Fish &
Seafood

> **6 medium trout**
> **salt and pepper, to taste**
> **2 tablespoons paprika**
> **1 cup pomegranate juice**
> **1/4 cup sugar, optional**
> **1 teaspoon cornstarch**
> **1/2 cup butter, melted**
> **1/2 cup finely chopped fresh tarragon or green onions**
> **3 lemons, thinly sliced**

SERVES 6.

Wash the fish inside and out, drying with paper towels. Make several incisions into the sides of the fish. Sprinkle the cavity and incisions with a combination of salt, pepper, and paprika.

While the coals are heating, bring the pomegranate juice to a boil and stir in the sugar, if desired. Cook for 10 minutes. If the mixture is not thick enough, just before serving the trout dissolve the cornstarch in 1 teaspoon water. Stir into the juice and cook until it thickens.

Place the trout on skewers. Grill the trout over glowing coals, brushing with a little butter and turning until the fish become golden brown.

Remove the trout from the skewers and pour a little pomegranate sauce over each fish. Garnish with chopped tarragon and lemon slices.

Fried Fish With Oranges

Narinchov Dabgvadz Tsoug

(THE ILKHANATE)

Fortunately, Armenians don't share the Mongol's lack of regard for fish. Their cooks have produced some genuinely original and enticing fish recipes. Here the blending of citrus flavors with fish, olives, and mint results in an unusual dish that is easy to prepare. Virtually any kind of fish can be used, but red snapper is common in Armenia. Feel free to experiment. I have cooked catfish this way with excellent results.

3 pounds red snapper or catfish fillets
salt to taste
grated rind of 3 medium oranges
salt to taste
1 teaspoon freshly ground black pepper
1 tablespoon paprika
1/3 cup all-purpose flour
vegetable oil for deep-frying
2 cups shredded lettuce leaves
3 large oranges, peeled, seeded, and sliced
1 cup pitted and sliced black olives
25 mint leaves
3/4 cup olive oil
1/3 cup orange juice, freshly squeezed and strained (about 1orange)
1/3 cup lemon juice, freshly squeezed and strained (about 2 lemons)
1 teaspoon garlic powder
1/4 teaspoon ground ginger

SERVES 6

Cut the fish into 3-inch-long pieces. Sprinkle with salt and rub the grated orange rind into both sides. Add salt, pepper, and paprika to the flour. Mix thoroughly. Roll the fish in the flour and deep-fry in oil until golden brown. Drain on paper towels.

Transfer to a warm serving platter covered by a bed of lettuce. Place the orange slices around the edge. Top the fish with the olives and garnish with mint.

In a blender, pour in the olive oil, orange juice, lemon juice, garlic, and ginger. Blend on high for 1 minute. Pour the sauce over the fish.

Serve with warm bread, finely sliced raw peppers and carrots, or a small side salad.

Persian Fish with Spinach, Rice and Herbs

Mohi Polou

(The Ilkhanate)

Fish &
Seafood

Both fish and spinach play important roles in Persian culinary traditions. Spinach is native to Persia and may have been introduced into China through the ambassadors of Khubilai Khan. This delicately flavored dish blends fish, spinach, and herbs with rice. The quality of Persian rice is arguably the highest anywhere, but is virtually unobtainable in this country. Your best bet is basmati or jasmine rice. Hybrids from Texas and California make an adequate substitute and have one advantage: they don't require rinsing.

> *2 pounds fish steaks*
> *garlic salt to taste*
> *1/4 cup vegetable oil or butter for frying*
> *1 teaspoon turmeric*
> *1 1/2 cups long-grain white rice*
> *1 cup finely chopped green onions*
> *2 cups coarsely chopped spinach*
> *1/4 cup finely chopped cilantro*
> *1/4 cup finely chopped parsley*
> *3 tablespoons finely chopped fresh dill*
> *freshly ground black pepper to taste*
> *1/4 cup butter*
> *1 tablespoon paprika*

Serves 4 to 6.

Dry the fish with paper towels and sprinkle lightly with garlic salt. Place the fish on a large plate and allow to stand for 15 minutes.

In a heavy saucepan, heat the oil and brown the steaks on both sides. Remove to a warm plate. Stir the turmeric into the oil and cook for 2 minutes. Remove from the heat.

Boil the rice for 5 minutes, drain, and turn into a bowl. Stir in the turmeric, green onions, and spinach. Add the cilantro, parsley, dill, and black pepper.

In a small pan, heat the butter with 1/4 cup of water until it boils. Pour half of this into the pan in which the rice was cooked, stirring and swirling to coat the sides and base evenly. Spread half of the rice and vegetable mixture in the base of the pan. Press gently with a wooden spoon so that the surface is flat and even. Place the fish steaks on top of the rice and pour the reserved butter over the top. Cover with the remaining rice. Over this, drizzle the butter from the rice pan.

Cover the pan with 3 paper towels. Then place the lid firmly on top. Cook over low heat for 45 minutes.

Remove from the heat and place the top layer of rice on a serving dish forming a ring, but leaving the center empty. Place the fish on a warm plate. Then spoon the remaining rice into the center of the dish. On top of this place the fish.

Sprinkle with paprika.

Salmon with Tomatoes and Herbs, Georgian-style

Tevzis Buglama

(KHANATE OF THE GOLDEN HORDE)

Fish & Seafood

This dish is a simple but tasty stew. Georgians, like Armenians, insist on their fish being fresh. During Uncle Ilya's travels across the Russias, he married a raven-haired Georgian beauty, also from a family of restaurateurs. When he returned to Moscow with his new bride, she shared this recipe with my grandfather. After my grandfather's death in London, the recipe was handed down to my mother and aunts and to me.

> *1 cup vegetable oil*
> *3 pounds salmon, skinned and cut into 1 1/2-inch cubes*
> *salt to taste*
> *freshly ground black pepper to taste*
> *3 teaspoons paprika*
> *1 1/2 cups finely chopped cilantro*
> *2 large red onions, cut into rings*
> *3 lemons, seeded and sliced*
> *6 medium bay leaves*
> *2 pounds tomatoes, sliced*
> *3/4 cup white wine*
> *1 teaspoon cornstarch, optional*

SERVES 6 TO 8.

Cover the bottom of a deep, heavy saucepan with 1/3 cup of the oil. Place the fish cubes on top and season with salt and pepper. Sprinkle with 1 teaspoon of the paprika. Add successive layers of cilantro, onions, lemons, and bay leaves. Pour another 1/3 cup of oil over the top. Sprinkle with another teaspoon of paprika. Then place the tomatoes on top and cover with the remaining 1/3 cup oil. Add a little more salt and pepper. Sprinkle with another teaspoon of paprika and add the wine.

Cover tightly and bring to a boil. Immediately reduce the heat to low and simmer for 20 minutes, or until the salmon is done. Stir in the cornstarch mixed with 1 teaspoon water to thicken, if necessary.

Fried Fish Slices
Chau Ch'ao Yu P'ien
(KHANATE OF THE GREAT KHAN)

Fish &
Seafood

Originating in the kitchens of the Forbidden City, where Pu Yi, the last Emperor of China spent his childhood, this tasty dish can be prepared with any white, firm fish. Long before the fall of Pu Yi, Khubilai Khan was the last Great Khan and head of the Yuan Dynasty. The first Buddhist Mongol emperor, he would often sample the fish dishes favored by his Chinese advisors, much to the disdain of his Mongol generals. A simple dish, it is bursting with subtle flavors.

> *1/2 cup cornstarch*
> *3 pounds fish fillets, cut into thin strips 1 1/2-inches long*
> *vegetable oil for deep-frying*

SAUCE:
> *3 tablespoons mushroom soy sauce*
> *3 tablespoons sugar*
> *3 tablespoons rice wine or sherry*
> *1 tablespoon rice wine vinegar*
> *2 tablespoons cornstarch*
> *2 tablespoons peanut (wok) oil*
> *2 tablespoons finely chopped ginger*
> *1/2 cup finely chopped green onions*

SERVES 6 TO 8.

Preheat the oven to 150 degrees F for 10 minutes before cooking.

Place 1/2 cup of cornstarch in a large nonmetal mixing bowl. Add the fish and toss until each piece is covered. Heat the oil to medium heat and deep-fry each piece separately for about 2 minutes. Set aside to drain on paper towels. Keep warm in the oven.

Clean the bowl. Mix the soy sauce, sugar, wine, and vinegar. Mix 2 tablespoons cornstarch and 2 tablespoons water, blend and add to the ingredients in the bowl. Mix thoroughly.

In a heavy pan, heat the peanut oil. Stir-fry the ginger and green onions for 30 seconds. Stir in the spice mixture from the bowl. Cook until the sauce thickens.

Remove the fish from the oven and place on heated pates. Pour the sauce over the fish. Serve with rice and a side salad.

Vegetables
& Grains

Rice Pilaf, Turkman-style
Turkman Plov
(CHAGHADAI KHANATE)

Crushed by the armies of Genghis Khan, Turkmenistan's history is inter-woven with that of the Mongols and their Persian and Turkish neighbors. The best Turkman food is never found in restaurants but in homes, where men, who rarely cook, take great pride in their traditional *plovs*, or rice pilafs, each considering himself an *oshpaz*—a master chef. It was from a gregarious, hospitable Turkman *oshpaz* that my Great Uncle Ilya learned the art of making *plov*, which he taught to my grandfather.

Vegetables & Grains

> *1/4 cup pitted prunes*
> *1/2 lemon, cut into 4 wedges*
> *1 medium onion, finely chopped*
> *2 carrots, peeled and finely chopped*
> *4 tablespoons olive oil*
> *4 peppercorns*
> *salt to taste*
> *2 tablespoons sultanas*
> *1 1/4 cups long-grain white rice*

SERVES 4 TO 6.

Soak the prunes in boiling water and add the lemon wedges. Leave to stand for 30 minutes. Meanwhile, fry the onion in olive oil until it becomes transparent. Cover with

2 1/2 cups water and add the carrots, peppercorns, and salt. Strain the prunes and stir them into the pan along with the sultanas.

Bring to a boil. Stir in the rice and reduce to a simmer. Cover tightly and cook for 15 to 20 minutes, or until the rice has absorbed all the water. Remove from the heat and let the mixture stand on a wooden block for 5 minutes, then fluff with a fork.

Serve as an accompaniment to *shashlyk* (page 98).

Imperial Mongolian Cooking

Tibetan Saffron Rice

Dresil

(Khanate of the Great Khan)

Barley is the staple grain of Tibet. Prior to the Chinese invasion, rice was a costly import that had to be carried from India across the Himalayas on the backs of porters. Not surprising, rice was a luxury item and a sign of wealth. In fact, one of Tibet's three most influential monasteries was named the Drepung, which means "rice mound," acknowledging its spiritual wealth and social significance.

Vegetables
& Grains

> *2 to 3 saffron threads*
> *pinch of salt*
> *1 cup long-grain white rice*
> *1/4 cup raisins*
> *1/4 cup golden dried currants*
> *1/4 cup slivered almonds*
> *1/4 cup honey*
> *1/4 cup butter*
> *1/4 teaspoon powdered cardamom*

SERVES 4 TO 6.

In a small, heavy saucepan, heat 1 2/3 cups water and add the saffron threads with the salt. Remove the pan from the heat and let it stand for 10 to 12 minutes until the water turns a deep, rich yellow. Wash the rice until the rinse water is clear. Bring the saffron water to a rolling boil and stir in the rice followed by the raisins, currants, and almonds.

Cover tightly and cook over a very low heat for 15 minutes. Meanwhile, blend the honey, butter, and cardamom. When the rice is done, stir the honey mixture into the pot. Cover and let it stand on a wooden block for 5 minutes.

Fluff with a fork and serve to accompany meat dishes and game.

Plain Rice, Mongolian-style

Budaa

(KHANATE OF THE GREAT KHAN)

Vegetables & Grains

Today, rice is in short supply in Mongolia since it has to be imported, usually from China and India. Mongolians most often serve steamed buns with their meat dishes, but rice is more highly regarded. This version uses basmati rice, a long-grain and aromatic rice from India. Most Mongolians will boil their rice in water, but the use of meat or vegetables lends character and color.

> *1 cup white basmati rice*
> *2 cups water, or clear meat or vegetable broth*
> *pinch of salt*
> *1/2 teaspoon oil or butter*
> *1/2 teaspoon paprika*

SERVES 4.

Wash the rice until the runoff water is clear. In a heavy small saucepan with a tight fitting lid, bring the water to a rolling boil. Add the salt and oil followed by the rice. Stir once. Reduce the heat to a simmer and cover.

Cook for approximately 15 minutes. Remove from heat and let the pan stand on a wooden block for 5 minutes. Fluff with a fork.

Sprinkle with paprika and serve.

Spicy Potato Curry
Shogok Katsa
(Khanate of the Great Khan)

Tibetan vegetables are usually grown in valleys, where it is warm enough to raise potatoes, mushrooms, radishes, and turnips. Because of the scarcity of potatoes, this dish is a specialty of wealthy landholding families. Tibetan curries are not overpowering like the curries of India, but are far more delicate and interesting.

Vegetables
& Grains

> 4 pounds potatoes
> 1 cup diced tomatoes
> 1 tablespoon crushed red chili pepper
> 2 tablespoons crushed garlic
> 1 teaspoon finely grated ginger
> 1/2 teaspoon turmeric
> salt to taste
> black pepper to taste
> 1 shallot, finely chopped
> 2 tablespoons vegetable oil
> 1/2 teaspoon fenugreek seeds
> 3/4 cup finely sliced green bell peppers

Serves 6 to 8.

Boil the potatoes for 35 to 45 minutes until they are done. Cool, peel, and dice into 1 1/2-inch cubes. Place the tomatoes, chili pepper, garlic, ginger, turmeric, salt, pepper, and shallot in a blender. Blend thoroughly.

Heat the oil in a heavy saucepan and stir-fry the fenugreek seeds until they turn a dark brown. Stir in the mixture from the blender and cook over high heat for 1 minute. Pour the sauce over the potatoes and mix. Garnish with bell pepper strips.

Serve with warm *kapse*, Tibetan fried bread (page 70).

Himalayan Potato Curry

Shogok Goptse

(KHANATE OF THE GREAT KHAN)

This version is popular among Tibetan nomads, whose diets consist mostly of meat. In summer they journey to Lhasa to trade and relax with bowls of hot potato curry, a rare treat. This version never appeared on our the London menu, but it was often found at the family dining table on festive occasions, where it was washed down with generous servings of ice cold vodka.

Vegetables
& Grains

> *4 teaspoons vegetable oil*
> *1/2 teaspoon fenugreek seeds*
> *1 tablespoon crushed garlic*
> *2 cups finely chopped onions*
> *1 cup diced tomatoes*
> *1/4 cup mushroom soy sauce*
> *1 teaspoon finely grated ginger*
> *1/2 teaspoon turmeric*
> *1/2 teaspoon powdered cumin*
> *2 pounds potatoes, thinly sliced*
> *1 cup water, or vegetable stock*
> *1 cup finely sliced red bell pepper*
> *2 cups finely sliced mushrooms*
> *salt and black pepper, to taste*
> *1/2 cup shredded green onions*

SERVES 4 TO 6.

Heat the oil in a heavy saucepan and stir in the fenugreek seeds until they turn dark brown. Add the garlic and chopped onions, stirring until they turn golden brown. Add the tomatoes, soy sauce, ginger, turmeric, and cumin. Stir and cover, cooking over low heat for 5 minutes.

Add the potatoes and the water. Stir and cook for 15 minutes. Add the bell pepper and mushrooms. Blend in salt and pepper. Cook for 5 minutes and remove the pan from the heat.

Sprinkle the shredded green onions over the top. Serve with rice or bread.

Spicy Cabbage, Genghis Khan

Baitsaa à la Chinngis Khan

(KHANATE OF THE GREAT KHAN)

This dish was introduced in Tibet by Mongolian warlords, who were eventually conquered by the peaceful ways of Tibetan Buddhism, which was introduced into Mongolia by Altan Khan in the sixteenth century. The dish has fallen into obscurity in Mongolia but is still enjoyed in Tibet. I have found the recipe works best when made with red cabbage. It makes a delightful side dish to lamb dishes and *dresil*, offsetting the latter's sweetness to create a harmonious, balanced meal.

Vegetables & Grains

4 cups diced red cabbage
1 1/2 teaspoons salt
1 cup diced onions
3 tablespoons vegetable oil
1 cup sliced mushrooms
1/4 cup sliced green bell peppers
1/4 cup sliced yellow bell peppers
1/2 teaspoon Chinese five-spice powder
2/3 cup water, or vegetable broth
1 tablespoon cornstarch
1 tablespoon mushroom soy sauce
1 tablespoon crushed red chili peppers, or to taste

SERVES 4 TO 6.

Spread the diced cabbage on a tray and sprinkle with salt. Push the salt into the cabbage by running a rolling pin over it. Let it stand for 40 minutes.

Meanwhile, sauté the onions in the oil until they become transparent. Stir in the mushrooms, cabbage, and bell peppers. Add the five-spice powder and stir. When the cabbage begins to soften, mix the water with cornstarch and soy sauce. Stir it into the cabbage with the chili pepper. Gently stir until the mixture thickens.

This dish makes a delightful accompaniment to a sweeter dish such as *dresil*, Tibetan saffron rice (page 165) or *zarda palau*, orange chicken rice pilaf (page 92).

Himalayan Split Pea Pancake

Seme Khura

(KHANATE OF THE GREAT KHAN)

Vegetables & Grains

A favorite in Lhasa and in the southernmost regions near the border with Nepal, this dish closely resembles a traditional Mongolian meat-filled pancake called *huushuur* (page 133). This version makes use of split peas and an array of aromatic spices. A sustaining meal, *seme khurat* can be eaten for breakfast or lunch, or served with dinner as a side dish.

> *2 cups split peas, green or yellow*
> *2 teaspoons crushed garlic*
> *1 teaspoon grated ginger*
> *2 shallots, finely chopped*
> *1/4 teaspoon powdered turmeric*
> *1/3 teaspoon powdered cumin*
> *1/2 teaspoon crushed red chili pepper, or to taste*
> *salt to taste*
> *1/2 cup finely chopped onions*
> *2 tablespoons all-purpose flour*
> *4 tablespoons vegetable oil*

SERVES 4 TO 6.

Soak the peas overnight in a large bowl filled with warm water. Drain off the soaking liquid and rinse the peas. Put them in a blender with the garlic, ginger, shallots, turmeric, cumin, chili pepper, and salt. Blend until smooth, adding a little water to the batter.

Pour the batter into a large bowl and stir in the onions and flour, mixing thoroughly. Adjust the thickness with water or flour. The batter should look like ordinary pancake batter.

Lightly oil a heavy saucepan (or griddle) and heat until very hot. Pour 1/2 teaspoon of batter into the center of the pan and spread it around. Then pour 1/2 cup of the batter into the middle. Again, spread it around until it is flat. Lower the heat and cook for 2 to 3 minutes on each side. Remove from the pan and place on a warm plate. Repeat the process until all the batter is cooked.

Imperial Mongolian Cooking

Ukrainian Potato Pancakes

Deriny

(KHANATE OF THE GOLDEN HORDE)

A fixture of the Ukrainian diet, potato pancakes can be made in large batches and stored in the refrigerator for up to 3 days. They are traditionally served with a dollop of sour cream. This dish was a specialty at our family's Moscow restaurant, which fell victim to the October Revolution. Fortunately, my grandfather was already in England and continued the family culinary tradition in London.

Vegetables
& Grains

1 large onion, grated
6 potatoes, peeled and grated
2 tablespoons all-purpose flour
2 eggs, lightly beaten
2 teaspoons salt, or to taste
1 teaspoon black pepper, or to taste
vegetable oil
1 pint sour cream

SERVES 4 TO 6.

Preheat the oven to 150 degrees F for 10 minutes before cooking.

In a large bowl, blend onion, potatoes, flour, eggs, salt, and pepper. Alternatively, use a food processor or a blender.

Oil a heavy saucepan and drop a heaping tablespoon of the mixture onto it. Spread it around and cook until it is brown on one side. Then flip it over and cook until the other side is cooked. Remove, place on a paper towel to absorb the excess oil.

Place on a plate in a warm oven. Repeat the process until all the pancakes are cooked.

Serve with plenty of sour cream.

Armenian Garbanzo Beans
With Spinach
Nivik
(The Ilkhanate)

Vegetables & Grains

Garbanzo beans form an important part of the Armenian diet and are used in a variety of dishes. This dish dates back to the Byzantine era and is one of many of the region's tasty preparations of garbanzos, which are high in protein. They remain a favorite throughout the Middle East and the former Soviet southern states.

> *1 cup dried garbanzo beans*
> *1 large onion, finely chopped*
> *1/4 cup vegetable oil*
> *1/4 cup tomato paste*
> *salt to taste*
> *freshly ground black pepper to taste*
> *1 teaspoon sugar*
> *2 pounds spinach*

Serves 6 to 8.

Wash the garbanzos well. In a nonmetallic bowl, cover with 8 cups of cold water and soak overnight in a cool place.

Place the garbanzos and the soaking water into a deep pot and bring to a boil. Reduce the heat, cover and simmer for 2 to 3 hours, or until tender. In a separate pan, fry the onion in the oil until transparent. Stir in the tomato paste, salt, pepper, and sugar. Mix thoroughly.

Wash the spinach under cold running water. Remove the stems and chop the leaves coarsely, then add to the garbanzo beans and the onion mixture. Cover and simmer for 30 minutes.

Vegetable Casserole, Turkish-style

Guvek

(The Ilkhanate)

In some regions of Turkey, *guvek* is served as a casserole with meat, in others it is a purely vegetarian dish. In either case, the flavor is always light and delicate. It makes a perfect accompaniment to grilled meats. My grandfather often served it as a main course with warm, freshly baked French bread.

Vegetables
& Grains

1 large eggplant
salt
4 medium zucchini
2 green bell peppers
8 ounces string beans
5 small ripe tomatoes, peeled
1/2 cup olive oil
3 small onions, sliced
1 tablespoon crushed garlic
3 teaspoons walnut oil
freshly ground black pepper to taste
1/4 cup finely chopped parsley
1/2 cup water or vegetable stock

SERVES 4 TO 6.

Preheat the oven to 350 degrees for 10 minutes before cooking.

Cut off the stem from the eggplant, peel off the skin, and cut into 1/2-inch cubes. Place on paper towels and cover with a layer of salt. After 30 to 45 minutes, a brownish dew will appear on the eggplants. These are the bitter juices the salt has extracted. Pat the eggplants dry with clean paper towels.

-CONTINUED-

Remove the zucchini stems and cut into 2-inch pieces. Cut the bell peppers into strips 1/4-inch in width. Cut the string beans into halves and slice the tomatoes. Heat 1/4 cup of the oil in a heavy saucepan and cook the eggplant until golden brown. Remove to a warm plate. Add the remaining 1/4 cup oil and heat. Cook the sliced onions until they become transparent, stirring frequently. Add the garlic and cook for an additional minute. Stir constantly.

Place a layer of eggplant at the bottom of a casserole dish oiled with 1 teaspoon of the walnut oil. Place half the zucchini, bell peppers, and string beans on top. Spread the onion mixture on top and cover with tomato slices. Dust with salt and pepper. Repeat the layering using the remaining zucchini, bell peppers, and string beans.

Sprinkle the top layer with parsley, salt, pepper, and the remaining 2 teaspoons of walnut oil. Add the water. Place in the oven and bake for 1 1/2 hours.

Serve with warm French bread.

Mixed Vegetables

Adzhapsandali

(KHANATE OF THE GOLDEN HORDE)

This Armenian dish resembles ratatouille with its lively blend of eggplant, tomatoes, and herbs. Unlike the more familiar version, *adzhapsandali* is hot and spicy, its bite coming from red chilies. A versatile dish, it is an excellent accompaniment to meat or game entrees. It is almost never served cold but is best presented steaming hot.

Vegetables
& Grains

1 large eggplant
1 large potato
1 medium onion, finely chopped
2 tablespoons olive oil
2 pounds tomatoes
2 tablespoons finely chopped garlic
1 green bell pepper, seeded and cut into strips
2 tablespoon finely chopped fresh dill
2 tablespoons finely chopped fresh cilantro
2 tablespoons finely chopped fresh parsley
2 tablespoons finely chopped fresh basil
1/2 teaspoon dried oregano
1 teaspoon salt
1 tablespoon paprika
1 teaspoon crushed red chili pepper
1/4 teaspoon freshly ground white pepper

SERVES 4 TO 6.

Preheat the oven to 375 F degrees for 10 minutes before cooking.

Prick the eggplant with a fork at 2-inch intervals. Bake for 40 minutes. Remove from the heat and allow to cool.

While the eggplant is cooking, boil the potato in salted water until tender. Drain, cool, peel, and cut into 1-inch cubes.

-CONTINUED-

In a heavy saucepan, sauté the onion in the olive oil until transparent. Drop the tomatoes into a pot of boiling water and cook for 10 minutes. Drain and plunge into a bowl of cold water. This should cause the skins to crack and slip off. Quarter the tomatoes and place in a blender until they become a smooth, creamy puree. Stir the tomatoes into the onions. Add the garlic and bell peppers. Stir in the dill, cilantro, parsley, basil, oregano, salt, and paprika. Simmer uncovered for 10 minutes until the mixture thickens.

Peel the eggplant and cut into 1-inch cubes. Add these to the pan. Gently stir in the potatoes, chili pepper, and white pepper. Simmer for 5 minutes.

Serve piping hot.

Beverages

Strawberry Lemonade
Yelagov Limonachour
(THE ILKHANATE)

In 1246, Pope Innocent's emissary, an aging Franciscan named Giovanni Plano Carpini, arrived at Karakoram, court of Guyuk Khan, bibulous grandson of Genghis Khan. There he found princes and dukes from every corner of the Great Khan's empire, including Armenia. During the Mongol Empire's days of conquest, Armenian soldiers rode at the side of Mongol warriors and forged military, economic, and cultural links between the two nations.

This is one of the most popular drinks made during the Armenian summer. *Yelagov limonachour* is also excellent as a cocktail boosted by a generous splash of vodka.

2/3 cup sugar, or to taste
1 cup lemon juice, freshly squeezed and strained (about 6 lemons)
4 cups cold bottled water
2 cups crushed strawberries
1 cup crushed ice

SERVES 4 TO 6.

In a heavy saucepan, combine the 1 cup tap water and the sugar. Bring to a rolling boil, stirring until the sugar dissolves. Reduce the heat and simmer 5 minutes. Remove the pan from the heat and set aside to cool. When the mixture has cooled slightly, stir in the lemon juice and bottled water.

Put 4 tablespoons of crushed berries in the bottom of each glass. Add a layer of crushed ice. Fill with the strawberry lemonade.

Tibeto-Mongolian Butter Tea

Tsai

(Khanate of the Great Khan)

This unique preparation is the tea of Genghis Khan's descendants. In Mongolia, it's called *tsai*. In Tibet, it's known as *boeja*. The Mongolian and Tibetan preparations of tea are essentially the same. They certainly conform to our Western notion of tea. Laced with yak butter and salt, Tibetans and Mongols drink anywhere from 40 to 60 cups a day from small wooden hand-held bowls. While not everyone's cup of tea, some Westerners enjoy this unusual preparation.

Beverages

1/2 cup black tea
10 cups hot water
1/2 cup butter
1 1/4 teaspoons salt
1 cup cream

SERVES 12.

Soak the tea leaves in hot (not boiling) water for 10 minutes. Boil for 5 minutes. Add the butter, salt, and cream. Blend for 2 to 3 minutes and serve.

Turkish–Armenian Mint Tea

Ananoukhov Tey

(THE ILKHANATE)

Popular in Armenia, Turkey, and Morocco, mint tea is often served after spicy meals. It is believed to help with digestion, even colds and the flu. Easy to prepare and always refreshing, mint tea is especially delightful to sip as the sun goes down on a balmy summer's day.

Beverages

2 tablespoons dried mint leaves
4 cups boiling water
pinch of saffron
4 cups hot black tea
sugar or honey, to taste
1 lemon, sliced into 8 pieces

SERVES 8.

Add the mint to boiling water and saffron. Steep for 5 minutes. Drain and mix with hot tea. Serve with sugar and garnish with lemon slices.

Tibetan Barley Beer
Chang
(KHANATE OF THE GREAT KHAN)

In Tibet, *chang* is most often made from barley, but wheat, rice, or millet can be substituted. It is best served hot with a little sugar added. Lhasa's best hotel, the Holiday Inn, serves its *chang* with honey. The results are delightful, especially if you can obtain leechy honey from a Chinese grocery. It's a little hard to come by but well worth the effort as the flavor is nothing less than ethereal.

Beverages

> 7 cups brewer's barley
> 2 tablespoons brewer's yeast
> 2 tablespoons sugar or honey (preferably leechy)

SERVES 12 TO 15.

Boil the barley in 15 cups of water. When cooked, drain and spread the barley on a clean surface until it cools. Meanwhile, put the yeast and the sugar into a food processor and blend until it becomes a soft powder. Sprinkle the powder over the barley and mix evenly.

Transfer the barley to a large sterile glass jar. Cover tightly and store in a warm, draft-free placed wrapped in blankets to hold in the heat. Leave it undisturbed for 3 days. If the barley has not begun to ferment, warm it a little. You will know when the barley is fermented by its odor.

Add 15 cups of fresh water and the honey. Stir, replace the cover, and set in the refrigerator. Let the *chang* age for 4 months.

When the process is complete, strain into a serving container through several layers of cheesecloth. Store in sterile bottles in the refrigerator.

Mongolian Milk Vodka
Airag
(KHANATE OF THE GREAT KHAN)

Beverages

The horse played a key role in Mongolian history. The fierce Mongolian cavalry cut through European armies like a hot knife through butter thanks to the speed and stamina of steppe ponies. Mongolians learn to ride almost as soon as they can walk. But the horse has another use—*airag*. In both ancient and modern Mongolia, *airag* is made from mare's milk. Its alcohol content is around 3%, but it is often twice distilled to produce *shimiin arhi*, which contains around 12% alcohol. Whenever one enters a Mongolian *ger* (a traditional round felt-covered tent), out comes the *airag*. To refuse would be gravely offensive to your host.

All you will need is 2 to 3 pints of milk (goat's milk can be used) and a steamer with several stacking layers. The bottom layer must be solid with the upper layers well perforated. The cover must be convex and placed on the top, facing down.

Place the milk into the bottom of the steamer. On top of this, place a perforated second layer. Place a bowl in the center of the second layer. Put the convex cover on top, upside down, and fill it with cold water.

Place the entire apparatus on the stove and bring the milk to a boil, but make sure that the top is sealed so that no steam leaks out. Reduce the heat and as the water in the lip begins to get hot, drop in ice cubes to bring the temperature down. Steam for 20 to 30 minutes.

When you remove the cover, the bowl on the second layer is filled with *airag*. You may repeat the process and double distill the *airag* if you wish to make *shimiin arhi*, which is usually served in small wooden or silver cups.

Imperial Mongolian Cooking

Russian Black Bread Beer
Kvass
(KHANATE OF THE GOLDEN HORDE)

Modern Mongolians picked up the habit of drinking beer from decades of Soviet control. Several brands of beer are available in Ulaanbaatar, including a pleasant brew called *Borgio*. Occasionally, one used to find *kvass* in Ulaanbaatar's hotel bars, but with the unlamented departure of Soviet advisors, *kvass* is becoming increasingly rare and resentment toward Russians and things Russian is on the upswing. Unlike *airag*, the Russian brew is a lot easier on Western stomachs and far more versatile.

1 pound Russian black bread
1 packet (1 tablespoon) dried yeast
1/2 cup sugar
1 sprig fresh mint
1 1/2 cups dried sultanas

MAKES 12 BOTTLES.

Cut the bread into small cubes and dry in a 250-degree F oven for up to 2 hours, making sure it does not burn. Place the rusks in a large mixing bowl and pour in 12 cups of boiling water. Cover with a clean cloth and let the mixture stand for 4 hours. Strain into a separate bowl through several layers of clean cheesecloth. Stir in the yeast and sugar. Drop in the mint, cover, and leave for 6 hours.

When the mixture starts to foam, strain it again and put it in sterile 10 ounce bottles, adding a few sultanas. Soak the corks in boiling water, which will make them quite flexible. Then stop the top of each bottle with a cork and store lying down in a cool, draft-free place.

Serve after 4 days.

Spicy Vodka
Spotykach
(KHANATE OF THE GOLDEN HORDE)

If Mongols and Ukrainians have anything in common it's their fondness for vodka, a beverage of Polish, not Russian, origin. While the best selling Mongolian brand is "Genghis Khan," a Ukrainian favorite is a home brew using an array of spices, one my grandfather reserved for special occasions to celebrate holidays with his circle of fellow expatriates.

> 2 pints unflavored vodka
> 2 cups sugar
> 1 tablespoon finely ground cloves
> 1 whole nutmeg
> 1 piece cinnamon bark
> 2 small vanilla beans
> 1 teaspoon saffron threads

MAKES 2 PINTS.

In a crockpot, warm the vodka. Stir in the sugar until it dissolves. Blend in the spices. Cover with a triple layer of cheesecloth held in place with a sturdy rubber band or a length of string. Place in a dark, cool, and draft-free place for 2 weeks.

Soak a few corks in warm water to make them more pliable. Strain liquid into sterile bottles through 4 layers of cheesecloth. When the mixture is free of spice particles, seal and store.

Serve after dinner in chilled liqueur glasses.

Spiced Whiskey, Ukrainian-style
Peperivka
(Khanate of the Golden Horde)

A traditional Ukrainian favorite, spiced whiskey is a pungent beverage. Take care in choosing the type of dried chili pods you use. Unless you enjoy your food volcanically hot, steer clear of habanero chilies and use dried Mexican *arbol* pods or dry mild Anaheim green chilies.

Beverages

10 dried chili pepper pods
5 cups whiskey

MAKES A STANDARD FIFTH.

Line the bottom of a sterile pot with the dried chilies. Add the whiskey, cover tightly and allow to steep in a cool, draft-free place for 12 days.

Strain and pour into a sterile bottle. Cork tightly and serve at room temperature or on the rocks.

Cherry Whiskey
Starosvitka Vyshnivka
(KHANATE OF THE GOLDEN HORDE)

Cherries are prized in the Ukraine, Armenia, and Turkey. No one knows how old this recipe may be, but some claim it originated in the twelfth century. While Russians and Mongols consume vodka in simple gulps, Ukrainians prefer to sip their liquor, using as a vehicle for conversation, not intoxication. My grandfather used it to prepare this rare Ukrainian recipe on special occasions and religious festivals for gatherings of friends and family.

> *4 pounds dark cherries, unpitted*
> *2 cups sugar syrup from equal portions of sugar and water*
> *2 pounds sugar*
> *1 whole nutmeg*
> *2 pieces cinnamon bark*
> *2 1/2 cups unflavored vodka*

MAKES A STANDARD FIFTH.

Wash the cherries thoroughly and place them in a large, sterile crock. To make the syrup, bring 2 cups of water to the boil and stir in 2 cups of sugar. Lower heat and simmer for 15 minutes, stirring constantly. Pour the fruit with the sugar, nutmeg, cinnamon, and syrup. Stir in the vodka with a clean wooden paddle. Cover with a double layer of cheesecloth. Store in a warm place for 3 weeks.

Soak a few corks in warm water to make them pliable. Then strain the liquid through several layers of clean cheesecloth. Store in sterile bottles, cork, and allow to stand for 5 weeks.

Serve after dinner in liqueur glasses.

Desserts

Uzbek Walnut Fritters

Samsa

(CHAGHADAI KHANATE)

Desserts

These traditional Uzbek fritters make a delightful finale to any meal. After visiting Samarkand in 1901, where he first tasted *samsa*, Great Uncle Ilya described the city as the "Jewel of Central Asia." The recipe became a fixture of the restaurant's menu and my favorite dessert. The scent of frying *samsa* brings to mind the legend and lore of Central Asia captured in James Elroy Flecker's poem:

> We travel not for trafficking alone,
> By hotter winds our fiery hearts are fanned.
> For lust of knowing what should not be known
> We take the Golden Road to Samarkand.

FILLING:

   6 ounces walnuts, pulverized in a blender
   1 1/2 tablespoons unsalted butter
   1 1/2 tablespoons sugar, or to taste

DOUGH:

   1 1/2 cups all-purpose flour
   2/3 cup lukewarm water
   1/2 teaspoon salt
   4 tablespoons unsalted butter

OTHER:

   vegetable oil for deep frying
   powdered sugar

SERVES 6 TO 8.

Preheat the oil to 375 degrees F for deep-frying.

Mix the walnuts and 1 1/2 tablespoons of butter with the sugar in a large mixing bowl.

In a separate bowl, pour in the flour. Make a well in the center. Pour the water into the well. Add the salt and 2 tablespoons of the butter. Stir until all ingredients are thoroughly mixed. Beat until the dough becomes firm.

Shape it into a ball. Lightly sprinkle a wooden board with flour and roll the dough into a rectangle 18 inches long and 15 inches wide. Brush the dough with 2 tablespoons of melted butter and fold into quarters. Roll it as thinly as possible.

Roll the dough into a rectangle 18 inches long by 15 inches wide. Cut into 2-inch squares.

Place 1 teaspoon of filling in the center of each square and draw up the corners until they meet in the middle. Moisten your fingers in water and pinch the corners to seal them. Fill the remaining dough rectangles in the same way.

Drop 8 fritters into the hot oil and turn with a slotted spoon until they are golden brown all over. This usually takes 3 to 4 minutes. Drain on paper towels. Fry the next batch.

Sprinkle with powdered sugar. Serve piping hot.

Mongolian-style Cake
with Creamy Icing

Byaluu

(KHANATE OF THE GREAT KHAN)

One of the more benign aspects of living under the Soviet thumb was that Mongolians acquired a taste for cake. The Mongolian cake tends to be on the heavy side, but this version is surprisingly light. Mongolian *byaluu* is covered with a rich frosting made from heavy yak cream. My grandfather's version is closer to but different from the original Russian recipe, called *bulka*.

CAKE:

2 packets (2 tablespoons) dried yeast
3/4 cup vanilla sugar (page 206)
1 1/4 cups warm milk
5 1/4 cups all-purpose flour
1/2 cup butter
3 eggs
pinch of salt
1/4 teaspoon powdered cardamom
1/4 teaspoon finely grated nutmeg

FROSTING:

3/4 cup heavy cream
2 teaspoons sugar
2 teaspoons lemon or orange juice, strained
1 egg white

MAKES 1 CAKE.

In a large bowl, mix the yeast with a teaspoon of vanilla sugar and enough warm water to make a paste. Stir in the warm milk and add 2 1/2 cups of the flour. Beat and cover with a cloth, leaving it to rise in a warm, draft-free area for 30 minutes until the dough doubles in size and becomes bubbly.

Melt the butter and add it to the dough with the remaining 2 3/4 cups flour, eggs, salt, cardamom, nutmeg, and the remaining vanilla sugar. Knead for 30 minutes and cover with a cloth, leaving it once again to double in size.

Line an 8-by-12 inch baking pan with buttered greaseproof paper. Knead the mixture lightly and transfer it to the pan. Leave for another 30 minutes to rise again.

Preheat the oven to 350 degrees F for 10 minutes, then bake for 60 to 75 minutes.

While the cake cools, whip the cream until it becomes stiff. Then fold in the sugar and lemon juice. Beat the egg white in a separate bowl until peaks form and fold it into the cream.

Cover the top of the cake with the frosting.

Turkish Delight
Lokum
(THE ILKHANATE)

Although fierce warriors, the Turks fell to the Mongol scimitar in 1243. While Turkish barley pudding was introduced into China through the Mongols, *lokum* never found favor with the khans.

Perhaps the best-known dessert of the Near East, *lokum* is eaten throughout the Moslem countries of Central Asia. *Lokum* can be flavored with lemon, orange, mint, vanilla, or rose water. The following recipe uses natural rose water, which can be found in supermarkets and in Asian groceries. Never use synthetics—they are made to emulate the fragrance of roses, not the taste. If natural rose water is unavailable, substitute two teaspoons of vanilla, mint, or almond extract.

> *4 cups sugar*
> *1 teaspoon lemon juice, freshly squeezed and strained*
> *1 1/3 cups cornstarch*
> *1 teaspoon cream of tartar*
> *2 tablespoons natural rose water*
> *2 to 3 drops food coloring, appropriate to the flavor used*
> *1/2 cup shelled and coarsely chopped pistachios*
> *1 cup powdered sugar*

SERVES 15 TO 20.

In a mixing bowl, combine the sugar with 4 1/2 cups water and the lemon juice. Stir into a heavy saucepan and cook over low heat until the sugar dissolves.

Raise the heat until the sugar water boils, then remove from the stove and rest on a wooden block.

Mix 1 cup of the cornstarch, the cream of tartar, and 1 cup of water in a separate pan. In a third pan, boil 2 cups of water. Slowly stir it into the cornstarch mixture. Heat the mixture until it becomes bubbly, stirring constantly.

Imperial Mongolian Cooking

Reduce the heat and cook on a gentle boil for 1 1/2 hours, stirring occasionally. Add the rose water and appropriate coloring. Blend thoroughly. Stir in the chopped pistachios. Remove the pan from the heat and place it on a wooden block.

Pour into a lightly oiled cake pan so that the mixture is about 1 inch thick. Let it set. The next day, mix the powdered sugar with the remaining 1/3 cup cornstarch. Cut the *lokum* into 1-inch squares.

Roll the cubes in the sugar and serve.

Desserts

Peking Dust

Li Tzu Fen

(KHANATE OF THE GREAT KHAN)

Desserts

Desserts are rare in China. This one was inspired by the dry, dusty storms that make their way every autumn from the Inner Mongolian desert to cover Beijing with a layer of yellow dust. When chestnuts were at their best around Christmas, my grandfather would buy kilos of the delicious nuts, peel and freeze them so this sumptuous dish could be offered at the restaurant year-round.

> *2 pounds chestnuts*
> *1/2 teaspoon salt*
> *1/3 cup sugar*
> *1 1/4 cups heavy cream*
> *4 drops vanilla extract*
> *12 pieces candied fruit*

SERVES 10 TO 12.

Make a 1/2-inch cut on the flat side of each chestnut. Bring a large pot of water to a rolling boil and drop in the chestnuts, lowering the heat to simmer for 45 minutes. Drain and remove the shells and skins. Allow to cool.

Grind the chestnuts finely. Place in a bowl and stir in the salt and half the sugar.

Whip the cream until it is thick and fold in the remaining sugar and vanilla extract. Form the chestnut mixture into a mound. Top with whipped cream and garnish with candied fruit.

Wine Gelatin

Dragli au Vin

(KHANATE OF THE GOLDEN HORDE)

A simple but delicately spiced desert, this Ukrainian favorite is a delicious way to end any meal. My grandfather's version uses lemon juice to cut the sweetness and spices to give the gel a character all its own. The recipe calls for white whine, but blushes and full-bodied reds give rich, satisfying results. You might want to experiment until you find the wine that's best for you.

Desserts

2 1/2 cups dry white wine
1 cup sugar
juice of 1/4 lemon, strained
1 tablespoon grated lemon rind
1/2 teaspoon finely ground cinnamon
1/4 teaspoon finely ground clove
pinch of finely ground cardamom
3 envelopes unflavored gelatin

SERVES 4 TO 6.

Place the wine in a stainless steel saucepan and stir in the sugar, lemon juice, lemon rind, cinnamon, clove, and cardamom. Bring to a boil and skim off the froth. When the sugar is completely dissolved add the gelatin. Stir until it dissolves. Allow to cool. Refrigerate for 2 hours and serve.

Mongolian Ice Cream

Marozhenaye

(KHANATE OF THE GREAT KHAN)

Ice cream is a rarity in Mongolia, but it does exist. It is surprisingly light and not too sweet. Occasionally, restaurants in Ulaanbaatar will feature ice cream on the menu. In reality, Mongolian ice cream is a Russian import adapted to local tastes.

Desserts

> **6 egg yolks**
> **3/4 cup sugar, or to taste**
> **3 3/4 cups whole milk or light cream**
> **1 vanilla pod or grated rind of 1 lemon**

SERVES 4 TO 6.

Beat the egg yolks and sugar, preferably with a wooden spoon. Put the milk in a heavy saucepan. If using vanilla, split the pod and add it to the milk. Raise the heat and bring to a boil. Remove the pan from the heat and let it stand for 2 minutes. Add the egg yolk mixture, stirring continually. Place the saucepan over low heat and simmer for 5 to 10 minutes, stirring constantly and making sure the mixture does not boil.

If lemon rind is to be used in place of vanilla, it should be added now. Remove from the heat and allow the mixture to cool. When the mixture is cool, transfer it to a nonmetal bowl. Fill a larger container with ice and set the smaller bowl containing the ice cream mixture in the center. Sprinkle a little salt over the ice. Whip the mixture with a whisk until it thickens.

Set the freezer to the coldest setting. Place the bowl containing the ice cream in the freezer. Whisk the ice cream every 30 minutes until it is half frozen.

Store in a plastic container in the freezer until ready to serve.

Sweet Rice

Chumi

(KHANATE OF THE GREAT KHAN)

Like the Chinese, Tibetans are not overly fond of sweets. Ironically, this recipe was introduced into Tibet by *ambans*, Chinese diplomats posted in Lhasa prior to the invasion of the People's Liberation Army in the 1950s. It then made its way to Mongolia, where Dorje passed the recipe to my grandfather. This version, his own adaptation, uses a variety of dried fruits and nuts. His British patrons loved the dish and it was always featured on the menu.

Desserts

> *2 cups long-grain white rice*
> *4 tablespoons butter*
> *1/4 teaspoon powdered cinnamon*
> *1/3 cup honey*
> *1/2 cup coarsely chopped walnuts or slivered almonds*
> *1/2 cup diced dried apricots*
> *1/2 cup dried currants*

SERVES 6 TO 8.

Toast the rice in a dry, ungreased saucepan for a few minutes. Then boil the rice in 4 cups water, reduce heat to simmer, cover, and cook until done, 15 to 20 minutes. Melt the butter and stir it in. Add the cinnamon and honey. Stir in the nuts and mix thoroughly. Place the dried fruit at the bottom of a large bowl. Pour the rice into the bowl and compress gently.

Lower the bowl in a steamer and cook for 5 to 10 minutes. Remove from the heat. Flip the contents onto a large plate.

Serve piping hot.

Tibetan Honey Rice Cookies

Khaptse

(KHANATE OF THE GREAT KHAN)

These delicately flavored cookies are always a part of the festivities on *Losar*, the Tibetan New Year. Baskets of *khaptse* are wrapped in silk to mark the special occasion. An alternative to baking is to fry the cookies until they are golden brown.

Desserts

DOUGH:

> *4 cups milk*
> *1/2 cup rice*
> *1 tablespoon (1 packet) yeast*
> *4 eggs*
> *1/3 cup honey*
> *1 teaspoon powdered cardamom*
> *1/8 teaspoon salt*
> *5 cups all-purpose flour*

SYRUP:

> *1/2 cup honey*
> *1/8 teaspoon finely grated nutmeg*
> *1/8 teaspoon powdered cardamom*
> *1/8 teaspoon powdered cinnamon*
> *1 teaspoon sesame seeds*

SERVES 10 TO 12.

In a heavy saucepan, slowly bring the milk to a boil. Stir in the rice and simmer over low heat for 20 minutes or more, stirring occasionally. Remove from the heat and cover. Let it stand in a cool place for 8 hours.

In a large mixing bowl dissolve the yeast in 1/4 cup warm water for 10 minutes. Beat the eggs and stir them into the mixture. Add the honey, cardamom, salt, and flour. Knead into a moderately stiff dough. Place the dough in a greased bowl and cover with a cloth in a warm, draft-free area for an hour until it doubles in size. Punch the dough down and knead for a minute or two. Form the dough into a ball then roll it on a lightly floured wooden board into a 1/4-inch-thick rectangle.

Cut the dough horizontally into 1-inch strips. Then make a cut down the center so that each piece is about 4 inches long. Make an incision into the center of each dough strip. Lift the strip from the cutting board and gently push one end of the dough through the center cut and pull it through. Straighten the dough and set it aside. Do the same with each piece and let them rise for 30 minutes.

Preheat the oven to 350 degrees F for 10 minutes before baking. Bake on a buttered tray for 15 to 20 minutes until golden brown.

Mix the honey, 3 tablespoons water, the nutmeg, cardamom, and cinnamon together. While the cookies are still warm and moist, brush each cookie with the syrup mixture, sprinkle with sesame seeds, and serve.

Barley Pudding
Belila
(THE ILKHANATE)

This recipe was brought to Mongolia by the hordes of Genghis Khan from their incursions into the Middle East and Turkey. It is customary to serve it after a hearty meal of Mongolian barbecued lamb. It can be served hot or cold, but in our family anything other than piping hot was unthinkable.

Desserts

1 cup pearl barley
pinch of salt
1 cup walnut pieces
1 cup sugar
2 cups milk
1/3 cup raisins
1/4 teaspoon ground cinnamon

SERVES 4 TO 6.

Wash the barley thoroughly. Place in a saucepan with 2 cups cold water with the salt. Bring to a rolling boil. Reduce the heat, cover, and simmer for 1 hour.

Blanch the walnut pieces by boiling them for 2 to 3 minutes. After boiling, strain and place the walnuts in a bowl of ice cold water. The skins should slip off, exposing the white nut meat.

Transfer the barley to the top of a double boiler. Stir in the sugar and milk. Cook for 3 hours on low heat. Chop the walnuts. Then add the raisins and nuts to the barley. Cook for 15 minutes.

Sprinkle with cinnamon and serve steaming hot.

Almond Custard

Keskul

There are variations of this dish throughout the former Mongol Empire, especially in China. This Turkish version is rich and alive with flavor. It was one of the most frequently requested desserts in our restaurants in Moscow and London. I greatly prefer it to the Chinese version for its character and deep, rich almond flavor.

Desserts

1 1/3 cups almonds
4 cups milk
1/4 cup ground rice
1/4 teaspoon salt
1/4 cup sugar
4 drops almond extract
1/3 cup toasted slivered almonds

SERVES 4 TO 6.

Blanch the almonds and grind in a food processor. Place the ground almonds in a mixing bowl. Heat 1 cup of milk until it boils and pour onto the almonds, stirring until blended. Knead into a firm paste.

In a separate bowl, mix 1/4 cup of cold milk with the ground rice. Heat the remaining 2 3/4 cup milk in a heavy pan until it boils. Pour over the ground rice mixture, stirring constantly before returning to the pan. Bring to a boil. Add the salt, lower the heat and simmer for 10 minutes, stirring occasionally. Remove from the heat and allow to cool.

Press the almond milk through a sieve and discard the grounds. Pour the almond milk into a pan. Stir in the sugar, return to the heat, and boil gently for 10 to 12 minutes.

Add the almond extract. Remove from the heat. Pour into dessert dishes and cool. Refrigerate for 2 hours. Just before serving, garnish with toasted almonds.

Glossary

Virtually all of the ingredients comprising the following recipes can be found in any major supermarket. Those items that are not routinely stocked by food chains can be found in any Chinese or Asian grocery.

Chinese mustard: Hotter than the American variety, it is readily available in the Asian specialities aisle of your local supermarket or in any Oriental grocery store.

Cilantro: Sometimes called Chinese parsley or coriander *(Coriandrum sativum)*, this flat-leafed herb has a strong but distinctive flavor and should be used sparingly in soups, meat dishes, and salads. Available in the produce section of your local supermarket. The use of cilantro was introduced into Chinese cooking by the Mongols.

Cinnamon: Available as dried bark or in powdered form, cinnamon *(Cinnamomum zeylanicum)* is widely used in drinks, desserts, and meat dishes throughout the East. Readily available in the spice section of any major supermarket.

Coriander: Comes from the same plant as cilantro, but refers to the dried and ground seed of *Coriandrum sativum*. Mild and aromatic, it is widely used in the Middle East and Central Asia. Coriander is easily found in the spice section of your local supermarket, but it can also be found on the Mexican food aisle (where the quality is just as good, sometimes even better, and the price is often lower).

Cumin: The strongly flavored seed of *Cuminum cyminum*, this spice is easily found in any supermarket or Asian or Latino grocery.

Dry mustard: The ground seed of *Brassica alba* or *B. nigra*, it is sold as a yellow powder in Asian groceries as well as American supermarkets. Often used in Chinese dishes and marinades.

Fenugreek: Sold ground or whole, the seed of *Trigonella foenum-gracecum* is an essential ingredient for many Tibetan meat dishes. Its availability in supermarkets is irregular. Your best bet is a health food store or an Asian grocery.

Feta: Available in any supermarket, feta is a Greek cheese from sheep or goat's milk. It's the most convenient substitute for the unobtainable Bhutanese cheeses that comprise *eze* salad (page 52).

Ginger: The aromatic root of *Zingiber officinale*, available in any supermarket, comes in a variety of forms ranging from fresh to chopped bottled ginger or powder. Introduced into Chinese cookery after the death of Genghis Khan.

Ground rice: Rice that is ground to a very fine powder. Used in Chinese and Turkish dishes, Asian grocery stores almost always have it in stock.

Mushroom soy sauce: A form of soy sauce flavored with Chinese mushrooms. Rarely found in supermarkets, it's a common item in any Asian grocery. Richer and more robust than ordinary soy sauce.

Nutmeg: The ground seed of *Myristica fragans*, nutmeg is a highly aromatic spice that is popular throughout Asia and should be used sparingly. It can be used to flavor beverages, meat dishes, and desserts. The spice counter of your local supermarket should have nutmeg.

Paprika: A mild, often sweet powder made from the dried peppers of *Capsicum annuum*, it is generally associated with Spanish and Hungarian cookery but also finds its way into Georgian, Russian, and Mongolian dishes. The best quality paprika is imported from Hungary and can be found in the spice section of your local supermarket.

Peastarch noodles: Sometimes called cellophane noodles, these fine threads are used in Mongolian hot pot dishes and are made from ground dried mung peas. They must be soaked before using; 15 or 20 minutes should do the trick. A popular item in Asian markets, peastarch noodles are cheap and easy to obtain.

Saffron: Subtle in flavor but not in cost, the threads of *Crocus sativus* are popular in Georgian and Tibetan dishes. Saffron was used to lend flavor and a bright yellow color to the crepes on which Khubilai Khan often dined.

Soy jam: Also known as soybean paste, it is often used as a dip for Mongolian barbecue. It is thick and dark. Sold in cans in most Asian grocery stores. Many major food chains now carry soy jam in the Asian food section.

Tamari: This Japanese version of soy sauce, unlike its Chinese counterpart, contains no wheat products and is suitable for those on a gluten-free diet. Most major supermarkets now offer tamari.

Turmeric: Sometimes called "the poor man's saffron" due to its bright yellow color, the taste of ground *Curcuma longa* is rather musty and should be used sparingly. Easily obtained in any supermarket.

Vanilla sugar: Not always available in supermarkets. To make, cut 2 vanilla pods in half and remove the seeds. Mix the pod and the seeds with 2 cups sugar. Store in an airtight jar. The vanilla sugar will be ready to use after 1 week.

Glossary

Recipe Index

Appetizers

Index

Beef

Beverages

Breads

Index

Desserts

Fish and Seafood

Lamb

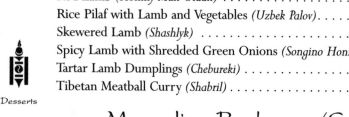

Desserts

Mongolian Barbecue (Sauces)

Mongolian Hotpot and Cooking Stocks

Poultry and Game

Salads

Sauces

Desserts

Soups

Vegetables and Grains

COOKBOOKS OF INTEREST FROM HIPPOCRENE...

Afghan Food & Cookery
Helen Saberi

This classic source for Afghan cookery is now available in an updated and expanded North American edition! This hearty cuisine includes a tempting variety of offerings: lamb, pasta, chickpeas, rice pilafs, flat breads, kebabs, spinach, okra, lentils, yogurt, pastries and delicious teas, all flavored with delicate spices, are staple ingredients. The author's informative introduction describes traditional Afghan holidays, festivals and celebrations; she also includes a section "The Afghan Kitchen," which provides essentials about cooking utensils, spices, ingredients and methods.

312 pages • 5 1/2 x 8 1/4 • illustrations • $12.95pb • 0-7818-0807-3 • (510)

The Art of Uzbek Cooking
Lynn Visson

A historical crossroads in Central Asia, Uzbekistan and its cuisine reflect the range of nationalities that form the country and continue to flourish there. This collection of 175 authentic Uzbek recipes includes chapters on Appetizers & Salads; Soups; Meat, Poultry & Fish; Plovs; Stuffed Pastries; Dumplings; Pasta & Pancakes; Vegetables; Breads; Desserts; Drinks; and even Suggested Menus.

278 pages • 5 1/2 x 8 1/4 • illustrations • $24.95hc • 0-7818-0669-0 • (767)

The Cuisine of Armenia
Sonia Uvezian

"Handsome, well thought out, clearly written, authentic."
—The New York Times

"...an exceptional cookbook ...A treasure that every adventurous cook should possess, one that a mother would hand down to her daughter and she, in time, to her daughter."   *—Hartford Courant*

487 pages • 5 1/2 x 8 1/2 • illustrations • $14.95pb • 0-7818-0695-X • (783)

The Art of Turkish Cooking
Nesret Eren

"Her recipes are utterly mouthwatering, and I cannot remember a time when a book so inspired me to take pot in hand."

—Nika Hazelton, The New York Times Book Review

308 pages • 5 1/2 x 8 1/2 • 0-7818-0201-6 • $12.95pb • (162)

The Art of Persian Cooking
Forough Hekmat
From creating a holiday menu to determining which utensils to use, this cookbook covers a wide array of practical information to help even the novice chef prepare elaborate Persian dishes. Includes over 200 recipes.
190 pages • 5 1/2 x 8 1/4 • $9.95pb • 0-7818-0241-5 • (125)

The Best of Russian Cooking
Alexandra Kropotkin
This array of Russian recipes also includes cultural insights and culinary tips to help you create your own authentic Russian feast. A survey of the tastiest offerings of Russian cuisine, this book includes popular dishes like *beef stroganoff* and *borscht*, as well as many lesser-known ones such as *kotleti* (meatballs), *piroshki* (dumplings with meat or vegetables), and *tvorojniki* (cottage cheese cakes). The 300 recipes are presented in an easy-to-use format.
288 pages • 5 1/2 x 8 1/4 • $11.95pb • 0-7818-0131-1 • (251)

The Best of Ukrainian Cuisine
Bohdan Zahny
This book presents both traditional and contemporary Ukrainian cuisine in an easy-to-use menu format. Ukrainian cuisine shares a common heritage with nearby regional cooking traditions, yet maintains its own unique character. Utilizing ingredients such as meat, poultry, fish, mushrooms, eggs, vegetables and fruits, these recipes cover the range of home cooking. Also includes a section on menu terms in Ukrainian and English.
304 pages • 5 1/2 x 8 1/2 • $12.95pb • 0-7818-0654-2 • (738)

Poland's Gourmet Cuisine
Bernard Lussiana and Mary Pininska
Photography by Jaroslaw Madejski
Here is Poland's cuisine as you've never seen it before! Bernard Lussiana, Executive Chef of Warsaw's celebrated Hotel Bristol, has taken traditional Polish dishes, like pierogi, golabki and flaki, and re-interpreted them in fresh, sophisticated and delicious new ways. Inspired by the beauty and spirit of the nation's lakes, rivers and plains, Lussiana takes bold new culinary initiatives with Poland's wealth of indigenous ingredients like buckwheat, poppyseeds, carp, pike, beetroot, suckling pig, wild boar, horseradish and dill, creating not only new dishes, but paving the way for a new era in Polish culinary history. Among the 52 recipes included are such exquisite offerings as

"Delicate stew of perch fillet, chanterelles and ceps flavored with marjoram," "Barley consommé served with quenelles of smoked game," "Pan-fried fillet of lamb served with a juice of fresh coriander and saffron kasza," and "Iced parfait flavored with zbozowa coffee."

Along with stunning, full-color food photographs of every recipe, are captivating photographs of the beautiful Polish countryside, and fragments of some of Poland's most evocative poetry. The recipes are provided in a step-by-step format and all adapted for the North American kitchen. A mingling of the senses—visual, artistic, literary, sensual and culinary—this book unfolds to reveal a dream of Poland rarely glimpsed.

143 pages • 9 1/4 x 11 1/4 • color photographs throughout • $35.00hc
0-7818-0790-5 • (98)

Polish Heritage Cookery, Illustrated Edition
Robert and Maria Strybel

• Over 2,200 authentic recipes!
• Entire chapters on dumplings, potato dishes, sausage-making, babkas and more!
• American weights and measures
• Modern shortcuts and substitutes for health-conscious dining
• Each recipe indexed in English and Polish

"An encyclopedia of Polish cookery and a wonderful thing to have!"

—Julia Child, *Good Morning America*

"*Polish Heritage Cookery* is the best [Polish] cookbook printed in English on the market. It is well-organized, informative, interlaced with historical background on Polish foods and eating habits, with easy-to-follow recipes readily prepared in American kitchens and, above all, its fun to read."

—*Polish American Cultural Network*

915 pages • 6 x 9 • 16 pages color photographs • over 2,200 recipes • $39.95hc
0-7818-0558-9 • (658)

The Best of Polish Cooking, Expanded Edition
Karen West

Now updated with a new chapter on Light Polish Fare!

"Ethnic cuisine at its best." —*The Midwest Book Review*

First published in 1983, this classic resource for Polish cuisine has been a favorite with home chefs for many years. The new edition includes a chapter on Light Polish Fare with ingenious tips for reducing fat, calories and cholesterol, without compromising the flavor of fine Polish cuisine. Fragrant herbal rubs and vinegars add panache without calories. Alternatives and conversion tables for butter, sour cream and milk will help readers lighten other recipes as well.

In an easy-to-use menu format, the author arranges complementary and harmonious foods together—all organized in seasonal cycles. Inside are recipes for "Braised Spring Lamb with Cabbage," "Frosty Artichoke Salad," "Apple Raisin Cake," and "Hunter's Stew." The new Light Polish Fare chapter includes low-fat recipes for treats like "Roasted Garlic and Mushroom Soup" and "Twelve-Fruit Brandied Compote."

248 pages • 5 1/2 x 8 1/4 • $9.95pb • 0-7818-0826-X • (274)

A Treasury of Polish Cuisine
Traditional Recipes in Polish and English
Maria de Gorgey

Polish cuisine is noted for its hearty and satisfying offerings, and this charming bilingual cookbook brings the best of traditional Polish cooking to your table—with recipes in Polish and English! Among the chapters included are Soups and Appetizers, Main Courses, Desserts, and 2 special holiday chapters—one devoted to "Wigilia," the festive Polish Christmas Eve Dinner, and one devoted to "Wielkanoc," the Polish Easter Luncheon.

148 pages • 5 x 7 • 0-7818-0738-7 • $11.95hc • (151)

Old Warsaw Cookbook
Rysia

Includes 850 classic Polish recipes.

300 pages • 5 1/2 x 8 1/4 • 0-87052-932-3 • $12.95pb • (536)

Old Polish Traditions in the Kitchen and at the Table

A cookbook and history of Polish culinary customs. Short essays cover subjects like Polish hospitality, holiday traditions, even the exalted status of the mushroom. The recipes are traditional family fare.

304 pages • 6 x 9 • 0-7818-0488-4 • $11.95pb • (546)

Hungarian Cookbook:
Old World Recipes for New World Cooks
Yolanda Nagy Fintor

These Old World recipes were brought to America by the author's grandparents, but they have been updated to accommodate today's faster-paced lifestyle. In many cases, the author presents a New World version of the recipe, in which low-fat and more readily available ingredients are substituted without compromising flavor.

This is more than just a collection of 125 enticing Hungarian recipes. Eight chapters also describe the seasonal and ceremonial holidays that Hungarian-Americans celebrate today with special foods: fall grape festivals; Christmas, New Year's and Easter; summer cookouts; weddings and baptisms. The book also includes culinary tips, a glossary of terms and explanations about the Hungarian language.

190 pages • 5 1/2 x 8 1/4 • $24.95hc • ISBN 0-7818-0828-6 • (47)

The Art of Hungarian Cooking, Revised edition
Paul Pogany Bennett and Velma R. Clark

Whether you crave Chicken Paprika or Apple Strudel, these 222 authentic Hungarian recipes include a vast array of national favorites, from appetizers through desserts. Now updated with a concise guide to Hungarian wines!

225 pages • 5 1/2 x 8 1/2 • 18 b/w drawings • 0-7818-0586-4 • $11.95pb • (686)

All Along the Danube, Expanded Edition
Recipes from Germany, Austria, Czechoslovakia, Yugoslavia, Hungary, Romania, and Bulgaria
Marina Polvay

Now updated with a section on classic Central European wines!

For novices and gourmets, this unique cookbook offers a tempting variety of over 300 Central European recipes from the shores of the Danube River, bringing Old World flavor to today's dishes.

357 pages • 5 1/2 x 8 1/2 • numerous b/w photos & illustrations
0-7818-0806-5 • $14.95pb • (479)

All prices subject to change without prior notice.
To purchase HIPPOCRENE BOOKS contact your local bookstore,
call (718) 454-2366, or write to:

HIPPOCRENE BOOKS
171 Madison Avenue
New York, NY 10016

Please enclose check or money order, adding $5.00 shipping (UPS)
for the first book and $.50 for each additional book.